ENLIGHTENMENT FROM THE SACRED PRECINCT

فيض الحرم في آداب وشرائط المطالعة وما يتعلق بها

Fayd al-Haram

Authored by
Ahmed Ibn Lutfullah Al-Mulawi

Translation and Annotation by
Mikaeel Smith

بِسْمِ اللَّهِ الرَّحْمَٰنِ الرَّحِيمِ

© 2019 Imam Ghazali Institute, USA
No part of this publication may be reproduced, stored in a retrieval system, or transmitted in any form or by any means, electronic or otherwise, including photocopying, recording, and internet without prior permission of the Imam Ghazali Institute.

Title: Enlightenment from the Sacred Precinct
ISBN: 978-0-9984380-0-9

First Print: December 2017
Second Print: January 2019

The page numbering of the second print does not correlate to the first print.

Author: Ahmed Ibn Lutfullah al-Mulawi
Translator: Mikaeel Smith
Proofreaders: Moosaa Khan, Aadil Cole, Husna Sattaur
Islamic Calligraphy: Courtesy of the Prince Ghazi Trust

Imam Ghazali Institute
www.imamghazali.org / info@imamghazali.org

Questions pertaining to the Imam Ghazali Institute may be directed to www.imamghazali.org or info@imamghazali.org.

This translation is dedicated to all students of the prophetic educational tradition and heritage. Those who tire themselves acquiring the legacy of Prophet Muhammad ﷺ.

Contents

Publisher's Message 9

Foreword 11

Translator's Preface 24

Author's Biography 28

Author's Preface 32

Author's Introduction 36

Section One: The general etiquettes for all types of researchers and students 45

Section Two: The etiquettes for those who intend to gain practical knowledge from their studies 61

Section Three: The etiquettes of learning for one seeking verifiable knowledge based on proofs 65

Section Four: An explanation of the specific etiquettes of the one whose intention is to gain the ability of retention by repetition 71

Section Five: An explanation regarding the etiquettes for one whose intention is to increase their knowledge or strengthen it from various means and sources 77

A Final Word: Regarding matters which benefit and facilitate in the attainment of what is sought after, from the perspective of perfection and completion 85

Conclusion: An explanation of group study and some of its conditions and etiquettes 95

Acknowledgements 154

About the Imam Ghazali Institute 156

About the Translator 158

Publisher's Message

The word pedagogy has its root origin in the ancient Greek language. The Greek word for child is *pais*, and leader, *agogus*. A *pedagogue* was therefore a leader of children. With time, the word pedagogue became known to mean teaching young children. In the greater context of the word and its meaning, it is about the guiding of someone towards an education and the educational process for the learner. Concern with the process of teaching and instructional methods developed in Europe significantly during the sixteenth and seventeenth centuries, yet within Islamic circles, pedagogical methods had been in deep discussion centuries prior.

When we think about Islamic education today, oftentimes we conjure up images in our minds of full time Islamic schools, seminaries, weekend adult schools, the Sunday madrassa, *maktab*, weekend intensives, and the list goes on. Similarly, we may also begin to think about the content or curriculum being taught. In a more immediate Islamic context, this would probably be *fiqh, aqidah, tasawwuf, seerah*, and so on. You may be asking yourself 'What is the importance of mentioning these?'. If we take a step back, we may quickly realize that one area that is often over looked in our madrassas, weekend intensives on *hadith* or *fiqh*, etc., is pedagogy. Pedagogy here refers to the way we teach and offer the instruction being imparted. A common issue today is that we focus on the building of institutes, weekend programs, and other types of courses that teach the subjects mentioned previously, yet we never discuss "how" to teach and study religious topics. Shaykh Mikaeel Smith's translation is important in this discussion because it represents just one example of a scholastic work in Islamic pedagogy.

It is our hope that readers of this book will benefit from the advice imparted to us by Shaykh Lutfullah. We believe that this text will elucidate some of the best practices on the manners and methods regarding the acquisition of knowledge. Though the methods that are spoken about by Shaykh Lutfullah ultimately seek to create the ideal student, teachers of the sacred sciences will also benefit immensely. May Allah bless the author, the translator, and the members of our team at the Imam Ghazali Institute.

I close by asking that should you, the reader and student, benefit from this text, please remember this needy servant and his family in your dua.

—Muhammad Adnaan Sattaur
IMAM GHAZALI INSTITUTE

Foreword

For those who spend significant parts of their professional or personal lives engaged with the Islamic intellectual tradition, with hours passed scanning page after page or pondering one page in depth, there are questions that not only go unanswered but oddly most often go unasked. For me, the most pressing is how the scholars who produced the voluminous works of *Hadith*, *Tafseer*, *Fiqh*, language and history could possibly have taken in, digested and reproduced such vast quantities of information.

Even in the modern day, with the aid of computers, databases and the internet, just trying to keep up with their work can occupy a scholarly career. How did those hundreds and hundreds of Muslim scholars who produced just the largest books in Islamic civilization go about studying, memorizing, looking up and referencing the ocean of details that they so skillfully sailed with such seeming ease? Every once in a while there are tantalizing hints: children in West Africa writing and rewriting the words of the *Quran* and, later, beginning books of law in charcoal on planks of wood; al-Hafiz Ibn Hajar mentioning how he wrote the *Fath al-Bari* by gathering a team of senior students, assigning each certain subjects to research and then meeting regularly with them to bring their contributions together. I wish I knew more about how these scholars undertook those feats of the mind and memory that daunt me daily in my own research.

Ahmad Ibn Lutfullah's *Fayd al-Haram*, translated here, provides a glimpse into how pre-modern Muslim scholars conceptualized the process of reading, understanding, retaining and employing knowledge. In that sense it is a valuable historical artifact for those interested in Islamic intellectual history – a relatively rare reflection, considered self-criticism and proposed solution to what the author felt were challenges facing students in his milieu. But the work is also useful across the many centuries that separate us from its author. It gives valuable lessons on how we think about reading, critically examining and classifying information. May God grant benefit to its author, translator and to us all through it.

—Dr. Jonathan A.C. Brown

* * *

THIS TEXT OFFERS GUIDANCE for a situation in which many students of knowledge find themselves today. Namely, reading works in the Shari'a sciences without access to our teachers. This book is for the intermediate student who has grasped certain usuli and logical concepts that help us understand the degrees of certainty on which evidences and proofs are built. In the shaykhs's words: "that student who is gradually proceeding through the stages of perfection by increasing [in his studies] day by day, little by little. This is what is intended by the term, 'intermediate student,' or one who is between the beginner and the expert." In terms of genre, this book should be read after Treatise for the Seeker of Knowledge by Imam al-Muhasibi which covers the adab and manners of one who is about to begin his journey in talab al-ilm (seeking knowledge).

The Arabic of this text was not easy. I would rate it as difficult - even more so in manuscript form - and because of that, students of knowledge should be very grateful that Shaykh Mikaeel Smith has been able to deftly translate it and present it in accessible English. This effort is also a testament to Shaykh Mikaeel's scholarship and grasp of the language.

I would like to highlight three simple, yet critical points that the author, may Allah shower him with mercy and blessings, brings up. In this sense, my contribution to this publication serves as a type of nut-shell summary of the cream of this work. The three points are:

1. Why the study of deen requires more caution than any other discipline.
2. The danger of self-study.
3. The guidelines for self-study.

The reader must know that the author, Shaykh Ahmad Ibn Lutfullah, an Ottoman scholar who took residence in Makkah, has brought up many more useful and interesting analyses such as: the essential elements of thought and thinking, the causes of stupidity, the tension between memorizing and thinking, the dangers of boredom and when one should stop reading, and the need for tranquility for the mind to function sharply.

Why The Study of the Deen Requires Caution

Disciplines are treated with as much caution as the missteps therein are dangerous. Misquoting a poet has very little 'real' consequences. Writing a bad novel has no negative impact on anyone except the author and the status of his income. As such, the field of literature is wide open for whomever can afford to give it a shot; it has no certification board. Shift now to bridge building, flying planes or surgery, and the matter is completely different. There is no room for incompetent people to slip through the cracks of those fields and endanger people's lives. The deen is one thousand times more critical than these disciplines. What people believe about the universe provides the foundations for a society's approach to all other fields, sciences, laws, customs and cultures. In addition to these worldly realities, errors in theology, as Imam al-Shafi'i noted, can kick off a series of events that ends with Hell-Fire, eternal or otherwise.

Consider the case of Barsisa the monk as an example. He made the fatal error of imagining that spiritual inspirations (ilham) were superior to revealed textual knowledge. Shaytan then wielded this against him, making him fall into the deadly trap of arrogance over the 'ulama, which led to distance from them, which in turn cut him off from knowledge. In time, Barsisa found himself entangled in an affair with a woman that resulted in pregnancy. Fearing the loss of his reputation as a saintly worshipper, he killed the woman. Fearing to be caught as a murderer, he obeyed Satan, who appeared to him with a deal: 'bow down to me and I will extricate you from this impending scandal.' At the end of a long and drawn out drama, the one-time saintly devotee to God ended his life having submitted to Iblis. But the beginning of the drama was one simple error in knowledge, namely failing to recognize that textual knowledge takes precedence over spiritual inspiration, without invalidating the latter as a source of clarification for the former, and that the slander of the 'ulama collectively, is in fact a slander of the religion itself and cuts one off from the greatest sabab (material cause) of salvation, sacred knowledge.

Barsisa's case may sound extreme, but that is only due to the extremes of saintliness, adultery, murder and the manifestation of Satan. But in essence, the idea of going astray into kufr is not uncommon at all. Consider how many thousands (if not millions) of believers were lost due to a similar error, namely that of Mirza Ghulam, a man whose beginning was in the circles of knowledge and whose end was in the claim to prophecy. He attracted a large following of believers and took them from claim to claim until he and they ended up in kufr. Worse, they coalesced into a formal community which resulted in their offspring also living and dying in the same kufr. How many lineages of iman were cut off by one man's delusions? Every renegade and heretical sect began with one man who may have simply suffered one mis-step in theology. This is why the field of sacred knowledge is so sensitive and must be treated with the utmost of care and caution.

Today, we find ourselves in a moment filled with critical thinkers, authors, speakers and activists that can amplify their voices and spread their ideas, while not necessarily appreciating the sanctity and sensitivity of theology, and the grave consequences of errors therein. Well-intentioned influencers may end up spreading misguidance without even realizing it. Allah tells us, "Shall I not tell you about the worst failures in their deeds? Those whose efforts were in misguidance, thinking they were doing good" (18:103-4). Worse, the mere idea of a dichotomy of guidance vs misguidance is often mocked. As a result, we find ourselves in the 'Wild Wild West' of Islamic thought, where no identifiable majority, university or canon can be found to offer any measure of stability. This is all the more reason for us to emphasize knowledge and equally important, the process of its acquisition.

The Danger of Reading by Oneself

As a general rule, reading the technical sciences of Shari'a without an experienced person to explain it is extremely dangerous for a number of reasons, logical and spiritual. Firstly, imagining that one has understood a text does not necessarily mean that they have in fact understood it as the author intended. In reading Sahih Muslim with my teacher, we would come upon many hadiths that were widely circulated and known. Further, we would spend much time reading the various chains and narrations of those hadiths. I shared an idea with the shaykh: why don't I read the chapter myself at home, then simply put a mark next to the hadiths that I didn't understand. The shaykh replied, "I'm not worried about what you don't understand; I'm worried about what you think you understand." We continued to go over every expression and meaning, and it was an exercise in respect for the text which was a symbol of the tradition as a whole.

The number of errors that a person can make reading on their own is unfathomable. To give an example, as soon as you buy a book, you're in essence vouching for the veracity of the publisher without even realizing it. One is engaged in an act of taqlid, blindly believing that the publisher was honest and accurate in their transmission. Publishing houses of Islamic texts should be treated with the same critical eye as transmitters of hadith. If the book is a translation, then it's double the effect, since translation itself is a form of interpretation, which is essentially scholarship. And so, before you've even cracked open the book open, you've placed your religion in the hands of people you have no information about, without even knowing it. This is why one's initial knowledge acquisition must be through living human beings whom the family or community have assessed and vouched for.

The second harm has to do with cutting off from the jama'a. Let us suppose, hypothetically, that an advanced student could read without misunderstanding. He or she knows the technical terms, studied logic and usul and benefits perfectly from their books. They would still be coming up short from another angle. Namely, that from the added benefits of the traditional person-to-person method of studying, is the idea of suhba. Self-study, even if extremely successful, can have the negative side-effect of cutting one off from the jama'a. Why go to a class, when I can read it myself in a shorter time from the comfort of my own home. Keeping the company of scholars is not solely about ensuring the accuracy of our understanding. It is also about maintaining pious company, which offers spiritual re-invigoration, moral reminders, exhortations and nasa'ih, and a strengthening of one's defenses against shaytan, who finds it easy to pick off the lone sheep, but immensely more difficult to attack a jama'a. A scholar alone may understand without error, but is nonetheless a fallible human being susceptible to the whisperings of shaytan who will work on his morals and behavior, getting him to slacken in observance. Good company protects from this.

The third type of harm is of a spiritual nature. The idea of seeking teachers and consulting one's peers has a spiritual effect, namely eradicating kibr. It has been said that no one becomes a scholar until they have studied with their elders, their peers and those younger than them. When they do this, they have proven their respect for the discipline over their love for their ego and its being superior to those of his generation, for the ego has no problem honoring the achievements of deceased scholars, but has great reservation in respecting its peers. Asking others is a humbling experience, in which one is essentially admitting ignorance on a matter. The refusal to corroborate one's understanding with a peer or someone younger can only be based in arrogance and kibr.

The Guidelines for Reading by Oneself

At what point can a student begin reading technical works by oneself? The author spends most of the book addressing this question. The summary answer revolves around the student's grasp over the following:
1. The different sources of knowledge.
2. The different types of evidences (speculative vs absolute, general vs specific, etc).
3. The structure of a sound argument (firmly establishing sound premises that lead to a conclusion).

Knowledge is derived from four sources: revelation, transmission, reason and observation (revelation in fact is a branch of transmission). If a student is firm in their epistemology, they will avoid many pitfalls, the worst of which can be kufr, while the least of which is the wastage of time. Often times, I come upon questioners whose iman has been shaken by the latest scientific theory. In such cases, I never discuss the theory, but rather, I begin explaining epistemology and the difference between direct observations and the theories that explain those observations. Scientific theories are never true or false. Rather, they are merely valid so long as they do not contradict any other evidences. But for believers, we also require the theory not to contradict revelation. No matter how impressive a theory is (be it scientific, historical, economic, etc), if it contradicts unequivocal revelation (i.e. a verse or verified hadiths whose meanings cannot be differed upon), then the learned believer rejects them on epistemic grounds. We must say: the Quran is right and the theory will eventually be disproven by evidence that has yet to be discovered. (Avid supporters of a theory are also resting on faith, namely the belief that contradictory evidence will not be discovered). As soon as a piece of information lands in the lap of a student of knowledge, he or she places it in one of the above four: is it revelation? Is it a historical transmission? Human reason? Observation? And so on.

Within revelation, not all of its texts are equal. Among the verses are as Allah says, "cornerstones of the Book, while others are ambiguous (mutashabihaat)." Ibn 'Abbas classifies verses into: "those which have only one meaning, and those that have multiple meanings." The second source, the Sunna, itself has various types within it. Between the mutawaatir hadith, the sahih and hasan hadiths, the 'amal of Madina, the fatawa of the Companions, and the action of the Companions, lies much discussion and debate among the mujtahid imams. Many fail to recognize that the sahih hadith has limits in the Hanafi madhhab (it cannot offer an exception to the Qur'an), while it is superseded by the 'amal in the Maliki madhhab. After the Sunna, comes qiyas (analogy), ijma' (consensus) and numerous other tools and the vast discussions that surround them. A strong basis in usul is a requirement in avoiding confusion.

After understanding the types of evidences and the system of deriving rulings, comes the structure of the argument itself. This is a sub-branch of mantiq (logic). The biggest error in this regard is the conflation between 'evidence' and 'proof.' Every text available is a piece of evidence. But that evidence must be now built into a solid proof. It is much like a crime scene, in which the police gather the evidences, while the prosecutor weaves the evidences into a case. A sound argument posits two or more absolutes that necessitate a conclusion.

In addition to these fundamentals of fiqh, essential for self-study, Shaykh Ahmad also gives practical advice. Among them is his warning that "digressing from one thing to the next is harmful because the one who does so becomes accustomed to a lack of attention." When a student chooses a book to read, after consulting with their teachers and peers about it, they should focus on it and not divert from it. Every time the thought comes to divert, he should say, 'what was my original intention?' If your initial decision turned out to be wrong, then how do you know that this decision is not also wrong? In this case, the person needs to go deeper and reassess their decision-making process. A teacher of mine once said, "The best book you read is the one you finish." Wandering from book to book, reading half a chapter here and half a chapter there is acceptable for leisurely or secondary knowledge, but not for the essential sciences of their chosen discipline, such as fiqh. For such works, the student is best off laboring through one book, not grazing through many. "The primary cause for students not reaching perfection is precipitance and not being patient…The primary cause of this is one's desire to raise their status in the sight of people and to gain acceptance from them." We also know that Shaytan himself will introduce the seeker to something good only to divert him from the good that he is already upon, so that he never completes anything. We ask Allah afiya and salama from this.

Conclusion

Sacred knowledge is a very delicate enterprise. The stakes are very high. In addition to caution in how we study, there must also be caution in how knowledge affects us, i.e. vigilance when it comes to arrogance, kibr, and relying on our own abilities. As the intention of this foreword has been to summarize the shaykh's arguments and extract its cream, I close by sharing some of his counsels:

> *"The student should travel from one continent to the next, seeking out teachers and scholars and not become impressed with himself or herself and their own ability.*
>
> *One should never desist from seeking more knowledge through taking it from the mouths of perfected teachers... going directly to them and seeking the benefit that is gained by sitting with perfected scholars, meeting them, and keeping their company. That benefit is one which can never be obtained by mere study.*
>
> *In regard to others, the student should have high opinions, both of those preceding the student, and those that live in the same time, seeing in them perfection and superiority, never looking down upon anyone because of their speech or apparent understanding.*
>
> *One should instead hold a skeptical opinion of one's self. One must be very careful to not become deluded by their own understanding and mental acumen. This will lead to him or her refraining from seeking out knowledge and participating in gatherings of*

knowledge. He or she will thus rely solely on their own ability to study.

Lastly, one must be completely and absolutely careful to not have bad manners in regards to one's pious predecessors because this is a major cause of one being deprived of reaching perfection.

We ask Allah for noble enablement and for good manners with our pious predecessors and our peers at all times."

Ameen.

—Dr. Shadee ElMasry

Translator's Preface

All praise belongs to Allah, the Lord of the worlds. May prayers and peace be upon our master Muhammad ﷺ, his family, and his companions, entirely. About ten years ago while scavenging through my mother's library of books, I came across an old book with an eye-catching title. Underestimating my mother's taste in literature, I had no idea that I was holding an original copy of one of the most widely read and studied books on education, Mortimer Adler's, "*How to Read a Book*".

At that time, I was studying in a traditional Islamic seminary and immediately recognized the value of this book. As I read through it, I fell in love with how the author taught the art of reading. Reading is an art and most certainly a skill, and needless to say, a science. I grabbed the book and told mother I needed to borrow it and take it to the *madrassa*. "*Boy, you better bring back my book!*" she exclaimed as I stuffed it into my bag. Book lovers know the struggle is real when it comes to lending books. After reading it cover to cover multiple times, I knew that this book was a literary masterpiece. But I wondered to myself if

Islamic scholarship outlined and codified the science of reading prior to this. My question was answered two years ago while I was researching Islamic pedagogical thought. I happened to come across an original Arabic manuscript from the twelfth century hijri written by the chief astronomer of Sultan Mehmet IV, titled *"Fayd al-Haram fi Adaab al-Mutala'a"* or in English, *"Enlightenment from the Sacred Precinct: A Manual on the Art of Reading"*. To my surprise, the work had never been translated into any other language, nor had it been published in Arabic. *Fayd al-Haram* stands in history a unique gem, that until now was nearly a lost treasure of intellectual thought in Islamic pedagogy.

Since the dawn of revelation upon the blessed Prophet Muhammad ﷺ, generations of Muslims have held learning and education to be a noble act of worship. Prophetic traditions enumerating the status of scholars are countless and well known to all Muslims. The inception of the final message to mankind upon Prophet Muhammad ﷺ was simply, *"read!"*. A command that has echoed in the ears of countless students and teachers, and inspired an Islamic pedagogical system that idealized culturing man through education and learning. Islamic pedagogy strives for ethical and academic excellence. This work is a small example of Islamic pedagogical thought and its detail.

Shaykh Ahmed bin Lutfullah penned this book towards the end of his life. Sitting in front of the *Ka'bah*, he wrote the text with the intention that it may serve as a source of revival of the deep analytical Islamic tradition in matters of education. Shaykh Ahmed was a polymath, having mastered multiple sciences where he was also seen as an official authority. He is known to have authored books in history, math, and astronomy. He states in the beginning of this great work that his main motivating reason for writing this text was the lack of attention given to the proper manner of perusing books or *Mutala'a*. His primary goal here is to teach and preserve the concept of "deep reading". It is my belief that "deep reading" of the classical religious texts has not only wavered but, in essence, died in many of today's schools. It could indeed be argued that studies are dedicated to a ceremonial teaching of books. *Fayd al-Haram* is a fresh reminder about the classical scholarly approach to learning.

Until now, students of Islamic seminars who searched for texts devoted to a correct method of acquisition would encounter books that focused heavily on the *adab*, or manners and etiquettes of acquisition. This includes how one should walk, eat, the order of stacking books, etc. And while we hold these as principles to follow in the highest degree, a student in today's context is heavily in need of a manual for the actual methods of reading and acquisition. In my understanding, the author's fear of a paradigm shift of the Islamic educational system away from critical analysis to a mere reading of the text has been realized. We have lost contact with the actual objectives of the trivium, and important sciences like logic are merely glossed at, if that. The author views the method of acquisition equally important as the content itself. The Islamic scholastic tradition is from one perspective anti-autodidact, giving extreme importance to formal education under a qualified scholar. The pedagogical methods that were spoken about by the Shaykh ultimately strive to create within a student a type of "readiness" or *Istidad* for independent acquisition of any science.

—Mikaeel Ahmed Smith
Maryland, USA
November, 10th 2016

Author's Biography

All praise belongs to Allah, the Lord of the worlds. May prayers and peace be upon our master Muhammad ﷺ, his family, and his companions, entirely. *Fayd al-Haram* was written in the later years of Shaykh Ahmed bin Lutfullah's life, in the year of 1691. He had been removed from his position as the "Chief Astronomer" and exiled to Egypt. Shaykh Ahmed bin Lutfullah was born in Salonika, Greece. His father, Lutfullah left his small Turkish town of Eregli to begin a new life in Greece. Within a few years, Lutfullah would be blessed with a baby boy whom he named Ahmed, born in the year 1631. From an early age, Shaykh Ahmed bin Lutfullah grew attached to the circles of knowledge. Sitting with the likes of Shaykh Abdullah, the grand mufti of Salonika, he excelled in Arabic, Islamic law, Prophetic traditions, and Qur'anic exegesis.

By the year 1654, Shaykh Ahmed bin Lutfullah was ready to further his education. He traveled to Istanbul, where he studied under multiple teachers in various areas. He studied philosophy, metaphysics, and logic under Shaykh Saib Effendi. He also studied under the leading astronomer of Istanbul, Muhammad Effendi. He spent the majority of his time studying and learning under the supervision of the spiritual guide, Shaykh Halil Dede in the Mawlawiyya zawiya. It is here that the reality of Islamic scholarship was realized for Shaykh Ahmed bin Lutfullah. Prophet Muhammad ﷺ stated in a well-known tradition that, *"the scholars are the inheritors of the Prophets"*.

The spiritual reality of knowledge should be transferred into the heart of its possessor, while in the stages of acquisition and study. This is the ultimate objective of studying.

$$اقْرَأْ بِاسْمِ رَبِّكَ الَّذِي خَلَقَ$$

"Read! In the name of your lord."

Shaykh Ahmed bin Lutfullah's intellectual strength and spiritual depth caught the eye of many in Istanbul. Upon the death of Chief Astronomer Muhammad Shalaby in 1667, Shaykh Ahmed bin Lutfullah was assigned to take up his post by Sultan Mehmed IV. It is very clear that Sultan Mehmed IV held Shaykh Ahmed bin Lutfullah's intellectual acumen and spiritual depth in high regard and eventually honored him with the position of *Musahib-i-Padishahi*, thus allowing him access to the innermost circle of the Sultan. When Sultan Mehmed IV was removed from his post in November 1687, Shaykh Ahmed bin Lutfullah was forced into exile in Egypt where his adopted son Morali Hasan Pasha served as governor. After some time, he moved to Makkah, where he became the spiritual leader of the local Mawlawiyya zawiya. Between 1693 and 1694, he moved to Madinah where he stayed for seven years. In 1700, he was recalled to Istanbul to work again as the chief astronomer, but declined the offer due to concerns of his age. He returned to Makkah for a final time, where he passed away on the 27th of February, 1702 CE (corresponding to the 30th of Ramadan, 1113 H). His tomb is located near the grave of our mother Khadijah (may Allah be pleased with her).

ENLIGHTENMENT FROM THE SACRED PRECINCT

فيض الحرم في آداب وشرائط المطالعة وما يتعلق بها

Fayd al-Haram

Authored by
Ahmed Ibn Lutfullah Al-Mulawi

Translation and Annotation by
Mikaeel Smith

Author's Preface

All praise is to Allah ﷻ who created within man the ability to study all the apparent aspects of existence in addition to creating within man the ability to contemplate the manifest signs embedded in it. Thereafter, praises are to Allah ﷻ for blessing mankind with the jewel of intellect, so that they may be guided by it to the core of what can be understood from that which is apparent. By this, we see that mankind may reach the unknown by means of the known. Prayers and peace be upon the most complete of those who studied, and the most observant, our master Muhammad ﷺ, the seal of the prophets and messengers. Prayers and peace be upon his family and his companions, who shined due to observing his splendor and being guided by his perfection ﷺ. May prayers be upon him constantly, and upon his companions and family.

Thereafter, this servant (holding on to the bounty of his mighty Lord ﷻ), Ahmed Ibn Lutfullah al-Mawlawi, may Allah ﷻ forgive and manifest kindness on him and his parents, begins with the following:

ENLIGHTENMENT FROM THE SACRED PRECINCT

My heart was troubled for some time. My mind continued to think of how previous scholars (may Allah ﷻ give them coolness in their graves) had such an abundance of love and mercy for seekers of sacred knowledge. They did not neglect any beneficial advice that would facilitate for them the means and methods of acquisition and learning. They expounded in detail upon all things guiding a student to his or her goal, all while providing scrupulous details of the ultimate reality. From this effort we see that they codified the rules of debate and discussion, allowing the development of both topics into independent sciences. Additionally, they authored many works in the sciences of debate and discussion and expounded on existing texts with their commentaries in addition to providing marginal notes. However, we find that scholars have yet to write exclusively on the manners and etiquettes of the acquisition of knowledge (i.e. how to study). Furthermore, the methods of acquisition and the levels of acquisition were never codified. While in reality, for the student of knowledge, knowing the art of acquisition and identifying the levels of acquisition are more important than knowing the science of debate. This is due to the art of debate being dependent upon one's ability to study. Every debate not preceded by proper study and research is in reality only arguing and disputing, and will only lead to embarrassment and prolonged regret. Perhaps one may suggest that the early scholars left this area to the understanding of the student, and trusted that one would learn the method of acquiring knowledge from the actions and examples of those who came before them. My reply to such a statement is as follows:

Had this been true, then it would have been more suitable not to mention the methodology of debate. Not only is it less important than the methodology of study and research, but it is easier to learn and master by studying the commentaries and the marginalia. Their love and regard for students of sacred knowledge was far too great for them to merely leave this important art for the student to learn on their own. In the end, everything is left to Allah ﷻ and only He controls the time in which all should happen.

While I was in this state of indecisiveness, I was studying one day and coincidentally came across a page where one of the earlier scholars mentioned some aspects of the methods of study. The majority of which were taken from the methodology of debate. However, it was not sufficient to cure the one in need or quench the thirst of the thirsty. So I added some of the things that I had learned from my own teachers and scholars. It then occurred to me that I should put together a short treatise, which discussed the methodology of study and acquisition of knowledge along with its conditions in a way that would assist the student in their journey and aid the seeker in their research.

However, a few things prevented me from pursuing this. Firstly, my nights were disrupted by much preoccupation due to changing circumstances in my life. Secondly, I noticed the lack of zeal in students and a restriction of their focus to only lowly things, which lay people desire. Thirdly, and perhaps the most hindering of all, was that I noticed my limited skills and my lacking ability. I said to myself:

> "Oh you incapable poor man! Are you at the level of writing and authoring you hold yourself to be? There is indeed an added challenge to writing in a genre where no one has preceded you with anything of benefit. Nor does there exist any written work to aid you in that which is difficult or that which is hidden from you."

Much time passed in this state. I would begin at one point and then become overwhelmed and stop. This condition continued until Allah ﷻ fixed my state by blessing me with closeness to the sacred precinct. Additionally, I was requested by some of the people of wisdom and nobility to embark on this endeavor. Due to the blessing of being in proximity to the sacred precinct and the truthfulness of the request, I overcame my hesitation, and relying on Allah's ﷻ help, the King, the All-Knowing, I began to compile a short treatise regarding the methodology of study.

This treatise contains a preface, five sections, and a conclusion. While writing, I continually begged Allah ﷻ to bring it to a good end. I named it *"Fayd al-Haram"* so that it may be known that the production of this book was not by any ability of my own, but only by the benevolence of Allah ﷻ and His gift. We ask for His inclusive grace and magnificent generosity that we make it for His noble sake, and that He make it beneficial for seekers of knowledge. We further ask that this will be a provision for us on the Day of Resurrection, by the sanctity of all the prophets and messengers, may the peace of Allah ﷻ be upon all of them.

Author's Introduction

Concerning The Division of Matters Necessary for Learning How to Study

To begin, one must know what *"mutala'ah"* or studying actually is. This includes the lexical meaning along with the terminology itself. The lexical meaning of the word *"mutala'ah"* is "to look at something". Generally speaking, (and by this I mean its common usage by the scholars) it is to look over or review a written work, seeking to gain a deeper understanding of it or something dependent on it. Furthermore, it is to look over written words, whose meanings are known, seeking to reach that which was intended explicitly by the author, or plausible. Studying is a science. It addresses the etiquettes of research and investigation along with the conditions of both. Its subject matter is the terminological meaning of *mutala'ah*.

Ultimately, the benefit is to protect the mind of the student from limiting themselves to outward meanings of written works and to prevent one from being deprived of the true realities and intricacies of a written work. The benefit of this knowledge is to use these etiquettes to increase one's ability to derive meanings from something. As for the objectives of knowledge acquisition, they are four. They vary according to the level of the student:

The student at this level has a good introductory knowledge of that which they intend on studying, but does not have practically applicable knowledge of it. For them, the objective is that they gain that knowledge (i.e., practical knowledge).

The student at this level has practical knowledge in relation to that which they are studying, although this knowledge is one of imitation. He or she has not learned from the perspective of proofs. Their objective while studying is that they should solidify that knowledge by understanding it through proofs.

The student at this level has solidified knowledge in relation to what they are studying. However, they are deficient in knowledge retention. Their objective while studying is that they reach a higher level by repeating that which they have received.

The student at this level has acquired, verified, and retained knowledge through studying, but such a knowledge can be increased. Their objective in studying is that they increase their ability and let it grow, by taking it from many places to strengthen their practical ability.

From this, we see there are four objectives of studying: to acquire, to verify, to retain knowledge (recall capacity), and to increase and strengthen. For each one of these objectives of study there are special etiquettes, just as there are general etiquettes of studying which will strengthen and help every one of the categories. For this reason, I have made the chapters of these groups into five sections. As for the benefit of this knowledge, there is something for every person who finds themselves on the path of studying; however, the majority of benefit will be for the common seeker of knowledge.

A student seeking perfection in knowledge will be one of three levels: the beginner, the expert, and the average learner. A seeker is in the beginning stages of knowledge when they are unaware of the methodology of studying and the methodology of deriving meanings from written works. The student at this level of learning should primarily take what they are seeking from the mouths of teachers because they are merely a beginner. As far as the one who has reached the later stages of studying, this person has obtained and perfected the ability to easily derive the deeper meanings of things presented to them without much mental exertion. This is the level of the expert seeker of knowledge. As for the one who is the average student, he or she has gained the ability to derive meanings, however, this ability is not completed nor perfected.

Moving forward, know that the term "ability" when used generally, describes a quality deeply rooted in a person. From this, a type of conscientious effect occurs with ease and without any deliberation. However, this is before it becomes a natural disposition. It is merely a temporal state which happens abundantly.

There are three levels that are sought after for the one seeking to perfect their knowledge. Each of these levels are a stage in the acquisition of knowledge. First is the stage of knowledge acquisition. This stage prepares a student for the next level:

extrapolating meanings, or the ability to deduce meaning. By means of this first stage, one gains the potential and readiness for the next stage: the deduction of knowledge. This capacity is obtained by learning the preliminary and introductory sciences of any field, and this is learned only through direct tutelage from a teacher. The goal and final objective of this capacity is to reach the next level, which is the capacity for the extrapolation of meanings. This first stage is the most general of all of the three abilities needed by a student. Second is the ability to extract meanings. It is an ability by which a person can derive meanings from anything which one encounters. One should be able to do this with ease and without any deliberation or force. This level is gained by the perfection of basic instrumental knowledge and by recalling the important topics discussed therein. The ability to extract meaning is completed and perfected when a person has not only a mastery in the extrapolation of meaning, but a surety without any doubt that what is obtained coincides with the real intent of the author.

Secondly, this condition should be in regards to all or at least the majority of fields and sciences. The perfection of this condition will be obtained when two qualities are found in relation to the science: mastery and confidence. This will be obtained by persistence and continuous study, taking into consideration all of the etiquettes and conditions of studying. Thereafter, one should compare that which one has derived to the extrapolations of other people who have mastered this level of study. One should meet them directly if they are accessible. Otherwise, they should travel to them, as this is the way of our pious predecessors. If you do not find such people in your town or elsewhere, [as is the case in our time today] one should say to oneself, *"verily we are from Allah ﷻ, and to Allah ﷻ do we return."* Thereafter, one should study and follow their footsteps and correctly follow what they have written, and contemplate their actions as well as their methodologies of extrapolation. One should similarly focus on their method of deciphering from one thing to another; how one entered into and concluded discussions, how one accepted and rejected certain things, how one digressed during discussion in a way that did not deviate from the primary intent, and all of the other ways which one navigated investigation. From this method, one should gradually advance from one science to the one above it, after he or she has perfected their ability to extract and deduce meanings with mastery and proficiency.

Due to the fact that the time it takes for one to perfect and master this capacity varies according to the acumen of the person, scholars decided to set the time it would take an average student to read, under a master teacher, a certain set of books from various fields as the benchmark for obtainment of this quality and its perfection.

Thereafter, scholars separated these sciences into introductory sciences and the core subjects, calling the one who completed this course *"Mukammilul Mawad,"* or "The Completer of Core Subjects." He or she is the one who has perfected and obtained the capacity to extrapolate meanings from those specific sciences completely and generally. After reaching this stage, the person is no longer in need of a teacher. One should busy themselves with increasing their knowledge and strengthening it through study, repetition, and teaching.

The third ability to be sought after is an ability to recollect learnt knowledge easily, and it is an ability by which one calls to recollection meanings and knowledge whenever one wants with ease, without any deliberation or force, and without the need to go back to the sources, be they books or individuals. This ability is mastered by repeatedly reviewing the respective sciences and their meanings until they are firmly and deeply established in one's mind to the fullest extent. This ability is completed when it is found regarding all sciences that are studied. However, it can also be in regards to a certain science specifically. This ability is the most rarified of all of the faculties, the highest of them in level, and the most difficult. When the term "expert" is used, it is referring to the one who has perfected this ability in all sciences, and in today's day and age, it is rarer than red sulfur. Likewise, when the term "master" is used in some sciences, it refers to the one who has the ability of recollection in that science, not the one who has the ability to extrapolate, nor the one who is at the stage of acquisition or obtaining knowledge. The usage of "master" for the one who can only extract meanings is figurative, in that the one who can extract meanings normally does so with the recollection of that knowledge. It is necessary for the seeker of knowledge that he or she spend most of his or her effort in obtaining the ability of recollection in their knowledge and they should not suffice on just acquiring the extrapolation of meaning even if it is perfected, because the master alone is the one who can recollect their knowledge.

There is no doubt that these three capabilities are sometimes in relation to just one question or topic. The first ability is that of acquisition. The second is the ability of extrapolation and meaning. The third is the ability of recollection and recall. Just as we have already mentioned regarding the four levels of students, these three capabilities can be general or specific to one science. Here, what we refer to is its relationship to all sciences amongst the scholars. From this, it should become clear that the majority of benefit in this science is for that student who is gradually proceeding through the stages of perfection by increasing them day by day, little by little. This is what is intended by the term, "intermediate student", or one who is between the beginner and the expert.

A student must also know the level of certainty and the speculative nature of the science they are studying. This facilitates successful attainment of their objective. Every student must have prior knowledge of the level of certainty and speculation possible for a particular science. This is so one does not seek out proofs for that which has no proofs, nor does one suffice on speculation in those areas where certainty is sought after. The highest level of certainty lies in the science of engineering because that which is produced from its premises is at the level of certainty and necessary. Thereafter are those knowledges which are gained of mathematical means. Such as basic math, surveying, algebra, balancing, astronomy, music, and others. The next level of certainty lies in the physical sciences and then the theological sciences. The physical sciences branch out to medicine and astronomy and so on. While the theological sciences (which are the highest type of speculative knowledge) branch out beyond theology and lay the foundations of jurisprudence.

After that, the science of grammar, etymology, and derivation of words will be found. As far as the science of language is concerned, there is a difference of opinion regarding it. Some people claim that language is not a knowledge because it is merely a word for terminologies and definitions. I object to such a claim by stating that the science of language includes claims, therefore it is a knowledge. Some people refute my claim by stating that these claims are specific premises or claims, but a knowledge must have general premises or claims. An answer to this counter-objection came to me, and perhaps it is not far from the truth. That is, the science of language has general claims, which are derived from examples, just like most of the Arabic sciences. This is supported by the fact that in every field of study from the aforementioned fields, there are general claims regarding language. As far as lexicology is concerned, there is a difference of opinion regarding it as well. Some state that lexicology is not an independent science due to the fact that it consists of only terms and definitions. I respond to such a claim by saying that lexicology contains claims, and this shows that it is a type of knowledge. However, this claim of mine is refuted by some who say that these claims referred to in lexicology are specific premises. Whereas knowledge is a term used for areas which have general premises. Consider this: every root word, from the root words mentioned in the books of language, are general claims, and every possible derived word comes from these roots. The roots have set meanings that do not change, for example, *"daraba zaidun"*. Thereafter, those roots are used to derive other forms. For example, *"daraba," "yadribu,"* and *"madroob."* By this, we see that lexicology is a science that is speculative, and it is used to derive examples in etymology and areas other than that of the science of Arabic language. We see that it is necessary for the one studying to take into consideration the levels of seeking out that which is impossible, or by sufficing on speculative knowledge in that which certainty can be achieved.

Section One

The General Etiquettes for All Types of Researchers and Students

It is necessary for every student to begin by mentioning the name of Allah and praising Him ﷻ. Then one should send their sincere salutations upon the Prophet Muhammad ﷺ, and recite the following:

$$\text{سُبْحَانَكَ لَا عِلْمَ لَنَا إِلَّا مَا عَلَّمْتَنَا ۖ إِنَّكَ أَنْتَ الْعَلِيمُ الْحَكِيمُ}$$

"Exalted are You; we have no knowledge except what You have taught us. Indeed, it is You who is the Knowing, the Wise."
al-Baqarah 2:32

The verse should be read to the end. Furthermore, one should recite whatever they have memorized from the narrated supplications so that they will gain blessings and enlightenment. One should also face towards the Qibla, which is a place of bounty, and they should humble themselves before Allah ﷻ, asking Him to bestow upon them the truth, inspire them to what is correct, to help them, facilitate for them that which they are seeking, and to make it easy for them.

Thereafter, when beginning a book in any field, the student should attempt to form a mental image of the science. This can be done by studying the common definition of that science. They should also understand the purpose and final goal of the book, and the objective of the topic so that he or she increases in their desire for gaining it, even if they are not a beginner in this field. This is applicable to anyone in pursuit of any knowledge and should be done even if they are not a novice to the science.

Thereafter, it is necessary for the student to conceptualize the topic by focusing on the introductory aspects of the topic and the intent or purpose. This is something done by everyone who is aware of the methods of study. A student must be aware of what it is he or she is intending to study. The lowest level of those capable of studying, are those who wish to gain a practical or applicable knowledge for which they have prepared themselves (i.e. having learned the introductory aspects). That "preparedness" is gained through the conceptualization of the entire science.

For example, the one who wishes to study or research the topic of the *"Existence of Primordial Matter"* to understand its reality and to explain it must know and understand that, according to the philosophers, there is something that is called *"Primordial Matter."* The philosophers claim that it is a substance and it exists independently. They further state that it has a body and there are other atoms and substances in it called "physical form." This is considered general knowledge which will create a desire to know the deeper reality of it, and to solidify that knowledge in depth and detail. One must then go back to sources that will contain the definitions and explanations from the books of philosophy. By doing this, one will gain a general understanding of the topic. Seeking these definitions of *"Primordial Matter"* from its sources will give the student the preparedness necessary to proceed. Then one can begin to study the actual topic in detail. One should start by correcting their pronunciation of the text (*ibaarah*) and cultivate a good understanding of the text by studying the individual words and sentence structures bit by bit. Through studying the individual words from the aspect of its root words and their lexical meanings, one will increase their knowledge of lexicology. By this, one will be protected from making mistakes from the perspective of lexicology. One will also begin to notice similarities and different aspects between lexical meanings and terminological meanings. Knowing and recognizing these similarities will produce other unanticipated benefits. The tendencies to notice similarities will, of course, be according to one's intellectual strength or weakness, and one's readiness to extrapolate meanings from other things. By studying the individual words from the aspects of its form, one masters etymology and will be protected from making mistakes, such as mixing up the forms of different words, which is very prevalent among students. The student will be able to differentiate between words in their original state and derived words, and that which is or is not a lexical analogy. Knowing the root letters gives one the ability to differentiate between that which is in its original form, and that which is not.

Perhaps by looking at the extra letters, a student may derive a subtler yet suitable meaning, and thus grow and strengthen his or her ability. Otherwise, if considered alone, the science of etymology is of great benefit, especially for protecting one from making mistakes. This is gained by studying the individual words from the perspective of the meanings of the words, and differentiating between the root words and the derived words, the general meanings from the specific meanings, the equivocal from unequivocal, lexical meanings from terminologies, and the figurative meanings from the literal meanings. Adhering to this method will give one a proficiency in the science of positing *(ilmul wad')*, which is the base of all sciences that are connected to sentence structure. If a person were to spend all of their time verifying the coinage of words and letters so that one knows the types of words and all three forms, then so be it.

After recognizing the set meaning for word forms, one must apply those rules to every word, taking into consideration the specific rulings that are connected to that type of word form, thus opening up the doors of study and investigation into the intricacies of the Arabic language. Thereafter, a person should begin an investigation of the sentences and parts of the sentences and how they are joined together. This study should be based on the rulings of grammar *(nahw)*, looking at the state of each of the words and expressions, and the *i'raab* that go appropriately with those words. This type of analysis will give a person a keen perception of the science of Arabic grammar and an ability to avoid confusion when coming across areas that are difficult for the one not proficient in sentence composition and organization. Normally, this happens to the one who has not mastered the science of grammar or one who is absent-minded, not taking into consideration the principles of grammar.

Through this type of studying, a person will open up the various subtle points regarding the intended meanings of phrases and individual words. After the opening up of these meanings, they can then move forward into a deep study in the actual subject matter that they are looking at. He or she can now run and roam through the fields of research if they are amongst those great horsemen of research. If they are not from amongst those people, even then, what benefit can there be above knowing good grammar?

Thereafter, one must study the rhetorical qualities of the words of the text. Different circumstances require an eloquent communicator to consider the most appropriate expressions needed to produce an intended meaning. This eloquence is often achieved by adjusting word sequence or alternating between specific and non-specific words. Of course, it is necessary that the written work itself be written eloquently in the first place. This is so the subtleties of meaning are clearly written and easily understood by the expert. These are some factors that masters of rhetoric might take into account, and masters of rhetoric have made this the central point of rhetoric.

Extended studying from this perspective will give one a mastery of *ilm al-maani*, or the science of meanings. One will gain an appreciation for eloquence in speech and rhetoric which will open up one's understanding of the subtleties of the exegesis of the Qur'an and the reality of the Qur'an. By this type of study, one also learns the method of gaining control of complicated meanings. These types of difficult meanings are called by the scholars of interpretation, "hunted or sought-after meanings." In contrast, the one who does not become familiar with this science and skill will remain clueless as to the best structure of words for achieving a particular objective. They will not have the ability to adequately express deeper meanings and feelings.

Then, one must review the written work to find if there are any subtleties of *ilm al-bayaan*, the science of expression. Such subtleties necessitate certain meanings or imply others. By this, I am referring to similes, parables, figurative speech, metaphorical speech, metonymy, or indirect expressions. In summary, one should look for any type of figurative speech in the written work. Extended studying from this perspective will give a person mastery over the science of expression, and this is the most important science for recognizing the miraculous nature of the Qur'an. One who does this will be gifted with an ability to recognize the subtleties of expressions and the subtleties of necessary and implied meaning written by the masters of rhetoric.

Taking note of the necessary and implied meanings of speech along with what can be learned from those meanings, individual words and phrases, root words, derived words, and corresponding words, the student then moves onto looking for secondary intelligible meanings. This refers to those meanings which are understood after the primary meanings have been understood.

This is the subject matter of logic, which uses the known as a means to reach the unknown. One will look at definitions first to see what types of speech they are, which include verbal, literal, nominal, complete terms, or deficient descriptions. Thereafter, one will analyze all of the parts of the definition to separate between the genus and the specific difference, and also separate between common accidents and particular accidents. The categories of things that can be known are based on the definitions of things.

One must study the various methods for dividing and categorizing through meanings and definitions. Such as when universals which are sub-divided into its parts, in which the whole universal term does not apply to each individual part of the category. Secondly, when universals are defined by subclasses. In the latter division, the universal concept can be applied to each and every one of the individuals of the group. The difference between these two categories is that in the first one, the whole is broken into parts which together form the whole. Whereas in the second one, the universals are broken down according to its different individual members. Then, one must look at whether these definitions are restrictive or non-restrictive, and whether the restriction (if there is one) is a complete restriction or mere inductive reasoning. Thereafter, one should also study all of the propositions and determine which type of proposition it is. Is it a singular or a compound word? Is it a real proposition or a conceptual composition, or an existent proposition in reality? Is it attributive or conditional? If it is conditional, is it conjunctive or disjunctive? If it is conjunctive, is it a mandatory conjunctive or coincidentally conjunctive, or is it a true disjunctive proposition, non-combining, or simply devoid? One will also look to see if it is individual or if it is restrictive. If it is restrictive, is it indeterminate?

In all of these categories mentioned above, one must see if it is a negative or positive statement. Then, examine the contradiction of this proposition and the equivalent conversion of it. Lastly, one must differentiate between the claim and the proof. One must begin by looking at the proof. Is it a type of syllogism, which is based on proof? Or is it a disputation syllogism? No proofs other than these three types (from the five types) are mentioned in recognized sciences, except very rarely. All of these go back to either induction or analogy, or continuation in preceding condition. Anything other than that which we mentioned gives nothing but speculative knowledge in any area of study.

If one recognizes a type of syllogism, then one must look to see if it is true, if it is coupled syllogism, or if it is an exception. They must also look to see phrases which logically lead to the result. Thereafter, one will look at which of the four forms they must take, take notice of the conditions of each of the forms, and see if everything is present. Then, they must see if it is complete, having all of the premises connected together or not. If it is incomplete by having only one premise (the major or the minor), one should question if this is due to the extreme clarity of the other premise or not. Sometimes, the proof is mentioned only as a sort of warning. If this is the case, one must look at the conclusion of the discussions to find out if it is a necessary conclusion. There may be a level of leniency in acceptance of the proofs. If one continuously persists in studying from this perspective, they will gain a great benefit. By great benefit, I mean the mastery and excellence in the science of logic. It is a mastery by which correct thinking is differentiated from incorrect thinking, and the best is differentiated from the worst.

And how could this not be the case, when the science of logic is the scale of intellect and sciences? The one who does not test their opinions and thoughts with this scale, their analogies and syllogism will not be correct, and they will be in loss. The one who does not sharpen their intellect and cultivate their mind with logic, their thoughts and perspectives will be full of mistakes. Logic is that which sets thinking straight, just as grammar sets the tongue straight. The truth is that these two noble sciences are two doorways for every student in reaching their perfection. So it is necessary for every student to strive and exert themselves fully to gain these two faculties and all that they contain, thus allowing them to use these in all of their studies and their research. One should not pay attention to statements that say *"logic leads to misguidance."* Rather, one should understand that this is mere ignorance and a type of blind following. Imam al-Ghazali, may Allah ﷺ be pleased with him, has stated in some of his works regarding the mandatory nature of learning logic for every person of intellect, and this is a balanced statement. After one has studied from this perspective, looking at the words and meanings, the first and second set of meanings, then one should now make a summary of the topic and all that it covers, from beginning to end. This will assist in making their knowledge solid. For example, one should say, *"the summary of this section is..."* or *"the gist of these words are...".* One may also say, *"the summary of this work is that it is known what the universe is, and it is known what non-eternal matter is. Then the ruling of non-eternalness is applied to the universe, and this is proven by change. Sometimes this is refuted, sometimes this is contradicted, etc. Sometimes these contradictions, objections, and refutations are responded to in such-and-such form."*

Thereafter, once a person has established the summary in their mind, they must think it over from every perspective and let their mind contemplate it many times so that it becomes very strong. Through this, they will gain a perpetual benefit from repeated study of the materials.

If it is difficult for someone to make a summary of the topic and to establish it in their mind, it may be due to various reasons:

1. A problem in the verbiage or wording. For example, a lack of clarity in the written work itself, which makes it difficult for one to specify the intended meaning. It could also be due to a mistake in the writing, a bad compilation of the words, incorrect grammar, or without consideration of the subtle meanings of compound statements and words. For example, one may come across a written work whose meaning is impossible to decipher because of the bad compilation from the author, or because of a weak correlation to relate it or join subject matters, and other things which make it difficult to understand and which make it hard for one to acquire the intended meanings. The only way to remove any difficulty in this type of problem (i.e. when the wording is difficult), is to look over the words and contemplate, try to decipher and adjust the

words according to their essence and meaning, and according to their compilation, until one finds in themselves clarification for their objections and for their misunderstandings.

2. Another problem may be from the perspective of meaning. For example, the meaning that one gets from the entire discussion is a very subtle meaning, either due to the reader, or it is subtle in relation to the work that he or she is actually reading. The difficulty that is perceived due to the subtlety in meaning is something which is obvious. However, the difficulty that is experienced due to uncommonness may not be, so we will explain what this means. The difficulty experienced due to uncommonness means that this meaning is not mentioned in books on this topic and is not familiar to specialists in this field, or it is well known to a specialist, but the reader is not acquainted with it. Another situation could be that the person is acquainted with the concept, but the manner in which it is stated, or the methodology which is used to explain it, is difficult. These types of difficulties are removed by repeatedly going over the text and constant study.

3. Another example of a difficulty in understanding the meaning is if the discussion is very long and has many branches. This can be due to the fact that the author is proving something through premises which in themselves have individual proofs. These proofs are connected to one, two, or even three other things. In any of these situations, there are many claims and many proofs. The

original statements become compounded with the derived conclusions. The claims and proofs become intermingled with one another, so a person becomes confused due to all the intermingling and overlapping. The reason is because the mind is simple. It flees from abundance when it is overwhelmed, especially if this abundance is confusing and unorganized. Indeed, the mind will only be able to conceive many things after it has solidified it from one perspective and organized everything into one form with a sequence that is understood, and it has put everything into one simple category. In both of these situations, the way of making it easy to understand is to differentiate between the original concepts and that which is derived from the original. Then, they must differentiate between the claims and the proofs, and also from secondary claims and their proofs. One must also put them in a natural order, and not look at a deduced branch before one has solidified the original along with its proof. Then, one will go to that which branches off naturally. They must completely ignore the mention of anything if it seems to be out of natural order. Rather, they should try to obtain a summary and make that firm in their mind, just as they did with the original. Then, they will go to that which follows naturally and do exactly what they did with the first set of information, and do this continually throughout the entire discussion. They should not go to another level until the first level has been solidified and they have separated the claims from the proofs.

By levels, we mean categories, the first of which deals with claims and proofs. The second level deals with learning the secondary proofs for the premises of the first proof mentioned to affirm the claim. The third level is learning the proofs for the secondary proof, and so on, until one reaches the necessary conclusion, or at the very least, the accepted conclusion. Regarding the second category, the first stage is looking at the stated proofs for the original claim and its associated claims. The second stage is to look at the associated claims and its proofs, and everything that is on the level of the associated claims. Thus, one can understand the procedure throughout the entire discussion.

4. Another cause of difficulty when studying is a lack of readiness in the student for extrapolation from that particular topic. A student should be ready for a science before beginning.

5. Having an unclear or clouded mind will also make studying difficult. This may be due to a natural quality in the student himself, or due to some external factor, such as an onslaught of thoughts and anxiety, or concerns. In this case, one should delay their studies until another time, because having clarity of mind and focus of attention is the fulcrum of any action. It should also be understood that for every time of the day there is a special effect, which cannot be found in any other time of the day. The sign of one being able to summarize the topic well is that the student is able to express the information in different words

and in more concise words than the original statement. For example, one may say to him, *"what is the gist of this speech?", "what is the summary of this discussion?",* or *"what is the point?"* In response one may say, *"the topic of affirming for every natural body a natural form, and the proof that comes with that."* The student would say, explaining the summary of the claim, *"The claim is that natural forms are found for everyone and the summary of the proof is that the commonality found among all things is the existence of finiteness. And the first thing that is being affirmed is general form. Thereafter, natural form is being established. The summary of the discussion and the question being asked is the unacceptable nature of the major premise from a secondary proof, and a summary of the reply to this is that the premise, which is refuted, has been established..."* and so on and so forth, until the end of the entire discussion. It is necessary for the student to contemplate over this summary after having understood the summary, and after it has become established in their mind.

One should now look over their summary, conducting a *"giving and taking"* session. This is done by placing the author in the position of one making a claim with proofs and placing themselves (the reader) in the place of asking a question. This method, however, is done by the student that has poor manners with their predecessors, like the one who says, *"they are men and we are men also."* What is better is that one places themselves in the position of the one seeking an answer and simply narrating a question on behalf of someone else. For example, one may say, *"what if someone refutes this way? What if someone objects this way?"* This is the method that is for one who has etiquette with the pious predecessors as should be the case. In fact, it is absolutely necessary because true virtuousness lies with those who came before us. Every writer from whom we benefit from amongst the scholars, they are in reality our teachers, and the right of the teacher over the student is well-known, as will be discussed in detail in the fifth section if Allah ﷻ wills. This type of give-and-take discussion is for the one whose intent is to gain, increase, or strengthen the ability of retention (*istihdhaar*). As for the one whose intention is to gain practical knowledge and to solidify it with proofs, this methodology of give-and-take is not necessary for him and what they are intending. Whoever has a clear mind and a good understanding such that he or she can depend on their own intellect, then there is no harm on this person to depend on their own faculties in acquiring what he or she is intending from practical knowledge and solidifying it. Then, after acquiring what one sought after, they should repeatedly study it until it reaches the level of easy recollection. However, the one who cannot depend on his own understanding and intellectual capability should not engage in such give-and-take discussions because it is not beneficial for them. Rather, it is disruptive to the order of studies and he or she will lose sight of what they intend to get. At this point, it is necessary for one to strive for the acquisition of knowledge and strengthening that which they know, and they will delay this discussion and debate to another study time.

It is necessary for every student or researcher to study the primary texts of those commentators who are trustworthy. One should depend on those in their extrapolation, and they should study their methodology, how they formed sentences, how they studied, and how they understood it secondarily. Then one should analyze how they open the discussion and investigation into the words and meanings. Likewise, when one intends to study commentaries from any field, they should follow a scholar who is accepted according to them and who wrote a marginal on that commentary. One should not study how authors wrote their commentaries, and then study how authors wrote texts, and then study both of those, and then judge between both of them. Rather, the student should study one aspect completely first and master that. If one does not have the capability to study from all of these perspectives in every type of field, they should then suffice by choosing that which is most appropriate and most important looking at their current state, and at the science which they want to study, and which is most important to them and their level. One should ask Allah ﷻ for noble enablement and for help to increase them. They should always repeat this prayer in their heart, both openly and quietly: *"Oh Allah ﷻ increase me in true, correct knowledge."* Truly He is the One who gives noble enablement. He is the Enabler, the Helper, and He does not deprive those who ask Him.

Section Two

The Etiquettes for Those Who Intend to Gain Practical Knowledge from Their Studies

After taking into consideration the etiquettes that have been mentioned in the first section. It is necessary for a student to think about what they are seeking in general from the science they are studying. Then, the student should consider the area of study they are looking at and ask whether it is beneficial and whether it corresponds with their general intention and purpose. If they find that it is beneficial and helpful to their general purpose, they must ask themselves the question: would simple imitational knowledge without proofs be beneficial, or deep, investigative knowledge be beneficial? If this area of study is one of the sciences which are auxiliary sciences which are not intended or sought after for themselves (i.e., etymology, grammar, meanings, expression, logic, literature etc.,), then there is no harm in simply sufficing on imitational knowledge.

This is because the discussions of these types of sciences are simply introductory concepts and set principles for sciences that are sought after in and of themselves. The characteristic of the fundamental introductory principles is that they should be accepted based on trust. Thereafter, when a person has gone to the second level of study, they can go further into the investigation regarding these foundational principles and the appropriate proofs for them. However, if the science which one is studying is a science which is sought after in and of itself, (i.e., the science of theology, the categories of philosophy) then it is necessary for a person to seek deep understanding and knowledge which is based on proofs. One should not suffice with only claims and imitative knowledge because if one does so they will be deprived of reaching their goal. However, if the area that one is studying does not have proofs, they should seek out the proofs from another source after having first made firm the foundation of that science through repetition. Then, one should study closely the proofs and their conclusions. The student should consider the benefit of the study with due thought, and they should practice the "give-and-take" discussions along with the rebuttal to potential questions as was mentioned in the first section.

The student must restrict themselves to one section and one topic in everything they are studying. They should review it time and time again. When the student has conceptualized the discussion from its beginning to its end, he or she should repeatedly think over the topic without visual aids, be they written words or diagrams. If one is not capable of only reviewing the meaning, then one has no other choice but to take help by picturing the letters which indicate to that already learned meaning. If one is incapable of that because of the closeness of the words, then one should annunciate to themselves the words. The student should not restrict him or herself to only one language if they are bilingual. Nor should they restrict themselves to the exact words of the source from which they learned. Rather, they should be able to articulate the meaning in their own words. The meanings of what you have mastered must become to you like an "old friend" that you recognize regardless of what he or she is wearing.

Your knowledge of that meaning or reality should not be restricted to one language, one specific expression, or one specific arrangement. The one who knows their knowledge or information in only a specific form has restricted their understanding of what they know and is called "a follower of the masses." This is something that not only causes stupidity and shallowness, but, is a sign of it. One should not mix up one topic with another topic while studying before having solidified the first topic and made it firm in their mind, even if there is a type of compatibility between them and they go together. This will cause confusion to the student, cause a deficiency in their learning, and stop the student from perfection. However, if one is at a level where they are mentally strong and their goals are high, it is possible to go through gradually, from learning practical knowledge to deep research or investigation, then to retention or memorization by repeating or by rote. Then, after that, one will not need to do a second reading to grow and increase what they know. Rather, this person will have reached that growth and strengthened their first reading because of the strength of their mind and high aspirations. However, if one cannot trust their intellectual capabilities in all of these levels of acquisition, investigation, and retention, one must use their eagerness, aspirations, and abilities in accordance with their strength. If a student has the capability to acquire, verify, and solidify the knowledge, but does not have the ability to gain the level of retention, they should do those two things and delay the acquisition of retention to another reading of this topic. However, if one cannot do all of them, then one should exert only in acquisition, and work to solidify what has been learned and make it strong in one's mind. Then, they will research and investigate deeper in another reading. In the third reading, they will work on their retention capability, giving each level its due. One should refrain from over-burdening one's mind with that which is above its capacity because this will cause one to desist and become bored with studies before reaching to perfection. We ask Allah ﷻ for enablement and help in every situation.

Section Three

The Etiquettes of Learning for One Seeking Verifiable Knowledge Based On Proofs

By this, I am referring to verification, or authentication of understanding, by learning the proofs for a particular subject. In order to achieve such a level of knowing, it is necessary that the student contemplate the subject matter. One must ponder if this knowledge is an auxiliary knowledge or if it is an intrinsically valuable science. If it is an auxiliary science, one must question whether it is based on proofs, or simply based on imitation and acceptance for that which there are no proofs. For example, the questions of grammar and some of the rulings of etymology and logic are based on proofs. Whereas lexicology, because as it was discussed in the first section, is debated whether it is a science in the first place. This is how the science of the Arabic language is viewed when one takes a light glance at the subject. However, it is in reality a science that is based on proofs from previous examples in the language. Now, if we were to consider it an auxiliary science which is not based on proofs, then the one studying it simply needs to gain proficiency and expertise by reading the trusted books in this field and from learning under the trusted experts. One does not need to busy oneself with searching for proofs. If it is an auxiliary science that has the capacity of verification based on proofs, then it is like other sciences (i.e., word derivation and etymology) and can be verified by learning other examples, similarities, application, and implementation of the correct guidelines. Such a categorization is supported by what is mentioned by Ibn Jini in his book *al-Khasaa'is*, where he narrates from his teacher Ibn Ali al-Faris that, *"analogical arguments are used in the science of language, just like they are used in the science of derivation of words and etymology and grammar, and from this, it becomes clear that if we need a four-letter word that has the root letters of dhaad, raa, baa, it is permissible to take it from another word paradigm by doubling the laamm kalima, or the third root letter based on the analogical argument, which is well-known even if this word is not known amongst the Arabs."* This is also proven in his book *Ma'rifa Mas'ala* where he states, *"to understand a question by the Arabic language through analogical arguments and to give preference to the conclusions found through such methods is better than memorizing a book and limiting oneself to listening and imitation."*

If a person is studying from the books of etymology, word derivation, and everything else that is based on these two fields, then it is necessary for such a person to refer back to a detailed text mentioning the appropriate guidelines for this science. One must then solidify knowledge of these principles and guidelines according to what is necessitated by the science being studied. If one is studying grammar, then it is necessary for that person to seek out the proofs and to verify their knowledge by reviewing the books which cover that field. In general, one must look closely at the proofs, whatever they are, in any field. This is done by looking at the proof and questioning whether such a proof has been passed down through narrations, or whether it is based on consensus, analogical arguments, breaking the analogical argument for a preference, or presumption of continuity. One should therefore look closely at each one of these types of proofs based on what is mentioned by Ibn Jini in *al-Khasaa'is*, as he has been exhaustive in his explanation therein. It is also recommended to read what is summarized by Shaykh Jalaluddin al-Suyuti in *Iqtiraah*.

If one is studying other auxiliary sciences that necessitate proofs, then seek these proofs out based on what is strongest, take the strongest proof, and duly contemplate over the premise of the proof, as was mentioned in the first chapter. If one's study is a science in which proofs are not sought after at all (i.e., the science of history, anthropology, literature, etc.), then one can simply verify these sciences and acquire expertise by memorizing its knowledge. If one would like to analyze these sciences, then extrapolate subtleties and new perspectives regarding the organization and formatting of the work. It is done by extrapolating figurative, metaphorical, and implicit meanings and taking into consideration the special attributes and aspects of rhetoric that are mentioned by masters in the field of rhetoric. The fullest extent that one can achieve in these sciences is accomplished by using examples and reference points to prove the perspectives that one is trying to show from the subtleties in the source. However, in studying the science of juristic principles, this is a topic with much room for debate and discussion. It is mentioned in the books of argumentation and debate and also in the conclusions of the books of jurisprudence. So, it is necessary for one to seek a proof for every question or problem within a question, and one must look closely at the proofs to do so. In regard to the sciences wanted per se, there will be three types: that science in which a proof is sought after regardless of whether the proof is from the rational proofs only, if it is from the related, passed-down proofs only, or if it is a combination between both of them.

1. An example of that which is based only on rationalism is the science of philosophy.
2. An example of a science that is based on passed-on tradition is *aqaa'id*, which is the science of Islamic creed according to the early scholars.
3. An example of the third science is *'ilm al-Kalam*, which is Islamic theology, or Islamic creed according to the later scholars.

The next category from the sciences that are wanted, per se, are those in which a proof is not sought after *prima facie*; however, it is sought after in reality. An example of this is *tafseer* (Qur'anic exegesis); there is no need for proofs in it according to what is apparent, but in reality when an exegete derives a meaning from the Qur'an, a proof will be asked in order to substantiate the exegete's statement. Such a proof will arise from that which is passed down by oral tradition or from the principles of the Arabic language. Only then will the derived meanings be accepted from the exegete and the *tafseer* considered acceptable. This is why *tafseer* is considered a science in which a proof is sought after, in reality. Similarly, in the case of the science of *hadith* (prophetic narrations), what is apparent is that there is no need for proofs in this science. However, when a *hadith* narrator attributes a saying to the Prophet, may the peace and blessings of Allah be upon him, he or she will be asked for a proof regarding the chain or narrators. Be it authentic, single-source well known, or strange, or any of the other categories of the chains of narration. If the *hadith* narrator connects the words in the text to the one who said them with an acceptable chain according to the scholars of this field, then it will be accepted. If not, it will be rejected. This shows that the science of *hadith* is really a science in which proofs are sought after and spoken of with respect to acceptance, rejection, criticism, and praise of the narrators of the *hadith*. All of this is well-known according to the scholars of *hadith*. As for the science of the principles of *hadith*, it is an auxiliary science and falls into the broader category of the principles of jurisprudence and is, in reality, a section of that science.

The third category is that group of sciences in which no proof is sought after outwardly. These may be from among the auxiliary sciences or they may be from the sciences that are wanted, per se. I consider this category to be tied more directly with the auxiliary sciences, like history and all the sciences of literature, because these sciences are studied by people of high aspiration.

Those who study everything from the sciences in order to perfect themselves because it is something beneficial to learn, or because it is useful for the perfection of beneficial sciences, such as *tafseer* or *hadith*, do not study this solely because it is enjoyable or attractive, according to those who enjoy studying the various sciences. From that perspective, it will be considered a science that is an auxiliary science, not a science wanted, per se, and indication has already been made regarding how one should study these sciences. As far as particular disciplines, the knowledge of which is considered praiseworthy information according to the scholars, each one of these will be studied according to the fundamentals of the general sciences from which they are based, regarding their rulings, their need or lack of need for proof, and their respective methods of study. And, we beseech Allah for His enabling grace in regards to the basis of knowledge and the branches of knowledge.

Section Four

An Explanation of the Specific Etiquettes of the One Whose Intention Is to Gain the Ability of Retention by Repetition

First and foremost, it is necessary for one to take notice of the similarities between that which one already knows and that which one is intending to study. This will be from the perspective of claims and proofs. If the person finds that there is complete conformity between the two in every perspective, then this is meritorious. However, if one finds out that there is some disagreement, then it will be disagreement either in the claim only, in the proof only, or in both of them together. It may also be a disagreement of the words only, the meaning only, or a disagreement of both. Secondly, in both of these situations, disagreements will be either complete or partial. These are the conceivable possibilities of difference. As for the possibility of disagreement in both claims from the perspective of words and meanings, it is inconceivable except in the case of a mistake. As for disagreement in words only, complete and partial differences are both conceivable. As far as a disagreement in meanings only, a complete difference is also not conceivable, though partial disagreement is possible. As for the proofs that words and meanings may be in disagreement completely or partially, this is because it is conceivable that a point may be proven through different proofs and methods. Similarly, in regards to the words alone or meanings alone, it is conceivable that they be completely or partially different. When both words and meanings are taken together, then complete and partial differences are conceivable only for the words. Whereas for meanings only, a partial difference is acceptable while a complete difference is not conceivable.

If a person finds a conceivable difference, then he or she must contemplate over the perspectives and circumstances of the difference until they can choose between the two sides and give preference to that which is stronger. If one cannot eliminate the differences through some type of preference and has the ability to retain both proofs, then one should strive to memorize both of them. Otherwise, choose the stronger of the two proofs and memorize it. While memorizing, it is also necessary for one to try and find a new benefit in the words or meaning of the text with each repetition. One should attempt to capture, in every one of their reviews, a new meaning from the untamed sought-after meanings, so that they will achieve two benefits through this method of study. The first will be the benefit of retention and the second will be the benefit of increasing knowledge. This will make the student from amongst the well-versed scholars.

There is no doubt that meanings contain deeper realities. Some of them are clear and some are hidden. The learning capacity of an individual varies in their ability to perceive and understand those meanings. Some students understand meanings quickly, others are slower in understanding, and some will never understand certain meanings because of its subtleness or their intellect, or due to a combination of both. Through this type of study, intellectual capacity becomes clearer, and one's level of scholarship becomes apparent.

By memorization, I am not referring simply to repeating the spoken or written words, or the meanings that go with those words. This is a skill which everyone who knows the definition of a given set of words is able to do. Mere repetition of the spoken or written words and their meanings does not increase one's intellectual capacity. One must know that there are two methods, or types, of repetition necessary for information to reach the level of acquired knowledge. One method is practical reading with application, while the second is reading and reviewing. This is because some knowledge that needs to be retained is auxiliary, and not intrinsically desired. These will be retained by repetition and looking over them and also by repeatedly applying them. For example, if a person wants to retain the knowledge of language, etymology, and the derivation of Arabic words, then he or she will study the books that contain this knowledge over and over. In anything that the student reads, mention will be made of the singular words and their sources and meanings. Then, mention will be made of the method of deriving one word from the next, followed by citation of its original form and the form that is derived from the original, along with those words which are derived through analogical reasoning, and so on. Likewise, if a person wishes to take his or her knowledge of Arabic grammar to the level of retention, they will study the books of grammar multiple times. When reviewing and repeating the rules and possible forms for any subject or text that one is reading, one should not be lazy in mentioning anything that is related to grammar in the text. One can apply this method to the sciences of meanings, expression, and logic, just as we have explained in the first chapter. As far as those sciences which are wanted, per se, they will be retained by studying and reviewing only. There is no room for application in these particular sciences, so it is necessary for this person to not skip from one subject to another until they have retained the first one sufficiently.

Likewise, one should not jump from one science to another until he or she has retained the first sufficiently. However, there are differences of opinion regarding the acquisition of expertise in a field. Does it refer to expertise in every single question relating to that field, or is it another type of expertise which one gains after having completed and perfected the science itself? Groups have gone in both directions, but my opinion is with the latter. One's knowledge or recognition within a demarcated area or a set topic does not mean one knows all of the particulars of that area. Rather, mastery of a field is a separate type of skill gained after being acquainted with all of the aspects of that field upon its completion. When it has become clear that mastery of a particular science is not the ability to master every single topic in that science (according to my opinion), it becomes necessary for a student seeking the faculty of retention to learn the science themselves. After having completed the study of all the topics of a particular field, one must analyze whether or not they have gained another type of mastery, i.e. mastery of the entire field. If they have gained that mastery, then this is excellent and it is that which was sought. If mastery of the field has not been gained, then the student must figure out what is preventing them from acquiring it. Is it due to an insufficient mastery of the various topics of that field or is it because of an inappropriate organization between the topics that were studied? If the reason is recognized, then it must be removed by any means.

There is an explicit difference between the one who has mastered the particular questions of a science and the one who has mastered the science itself. The difference is, when the one who has mastered the questions of a science without mastering the science itself is asked about the science, they typically do not have general comprehensive knowledge of every single question, whereas the one who has mastered the questions and particulars along with the science itself, does. If one is asked about the science itself, one will have a general comprehensive understanding of all of the questions of the science and will be able to digress into details when questioned further. It is as if, for this person, the entire science is one comprehensive question which is comprised of different sciences and knowledge, as has been explained. This is the most exemplary and highest form of knowledge that one must have pertaining to the particulars. This knowledge is the connecting point between general knowledge and particular, specific knowledge. So the discussion is not about which knowledge a person should focus on, but rather, how they should be brought together. Yes, it is true that if the one who only possesses knowledge of the particulars is asked about every topic and question in that field, then they will have knowledge of many of the questions that were asked. However, when such a person is asked about the entire comprehensive science, then they will not have the ability to answer.

We have now made this matter clear, and it is extremely important to be vigilant of this. There are many benefits of knowledge which branch off of this point. One must always say *"my Lord increase me in beneficial knowledge."*

Section Five

An Explanation Regarding the Etiquettes for One Whose Intention Is to Increase Their Knowledge or Strengthen It from Various Means and Sources

As far as the first is concerned, i.e., increasing one's knowledge, this is something which is conceivable and something that can be done, as agreed upon by all of the scholars. As far as the second is concerned, which is strengthening knowledge, it is agreed upon in regards to affirming its possibility. However, there is disagreement regarding its possibility from the standpoint of apprehension.

The opinion of the great Imam, Abu Hanifah, is that apprehension is something, which does not have the capability of being strengthened or weakened. He claims that an unknown is always unknown and it can never be known. He attempted to prove this position by saying that if something is known from any perspective and then it is learned again from another perspective, then the knowledge has been multiplied, not strengthened. Knowledge from the first perspective is one specific type of knowledge, and knowledge from the second perspective is another specific type of knowledge different than the first. Thus, we see that knowledge is multiplied and not strengthened. If this statement were true, then it would not be possible to know anything. This is an example of circular reasoning, because if a certain thing is assumed to be known from one perspective, then what is actually known is the perspective and not the thing itself. Moreover, the connection between the thing that is unknown and the taken perspective is also unknown. Because the knowledge of the connection is dependent upon knowledge of the thing itself, this is clearly circular reasoning. The great researcher, Nasir al-Deen al-Tusi, differed from Abu Hanifah's opinion in his book *Awaahil Sharhul Ishaaraat*, in which he said:

"Indeed the great researcher and commentator erred in that he did not differentiate between that which is known and visible and whose essence is knowable, and that which is known and visible secondarily. If someone conceptualizes something from any perspective, it is the thing and not the perspective that one is conceptualizing. The perspective is conceptualized and noticeable only secondarily. Thereafter, the perspective is only conceptualized to serve as a reflection or mirror for the conceptualization of the thing whose essence is noticeable. Our conceptualization of that thing from a different perspective strengthens our conceptualization of the actual thing itself. From this, it becomes clear that we can see that knowledge, or conceptualization (apprehensive knowledge), be increased by the different perspectives by which a thing is studied."

This is a summary of the words of Nasir al-Deen al-Tusi, which is in my estimation the most acceptable position. As for strengthening one's affirmation and perfection, it is agreed upon by all scholars as being conceivable. There is no doubt that when a judgement is proven by one proof and confirmed by another proof, the result is an increase and solidifying of that knowledge. This being the case, we say it is necessary for a person who is mastering a field or a particular topic, or any person mastering any type of practical knowledge, to completely exert oneself, first and foremost. Gaining and strengthening one's knowledge is done through digressing correctly into the areas which are intrinsically connected, and thereafter all of the extremities of these areas. This is done by obtaining more knowledge from multiple, different sources. Thereafter, one should think over the topic regarding its apprehensions and affirmations. Are there any questions that remain unsolved? If there is something which is unresolved, is it possible for it to be fixed or not? If one does not find anything that is objectionable at all, this can either be due to some level of perfection within one's self or the author. This is indeed a great finding and one should be grateful for achieving this. However, it can also be a result of a deficiency in the student. This deficiency is either due to a topical study of the various connected fields of the subject, or a failure to give due attention to the writing and terminology used and the formulated sentences. It can also be due to a deficiency in one's study of the topic and the inability to comprehend all of its parts, conditions, and limits. Or, by having poorly summarized the materials the first time they were studied.

Thereafter, the initial inaccurate summary became firm in one's mind. The remedy for all this is simply continual revision and review of the subject generally at first, and secondly with detail and precision, both with the words and the meanings, until one achieves that which is sought after due to the blessing of time and circumstance. When one has obtained what they are seeking, either in the beginning or after many repetitions, the next step is that one must put the author in the position of a claimant and put themselves in the position of an investigator, as was explained in the first section.

One must audibly speak to oneself with words as if seeking answers from a question, or one may narrate questions to the author as if someone else is asking the question. For example, *"If a person objects by saying such-and-such a statement, what would you say in reply?"* One may also pretend as if one is debating with someone that holds a conflicting opinion. In this case, one will give replies from the perspective of the author by using the evidence and statements that the author has given and mentioned. One will continue to increase in the investigation, as well as questioning and answering, in accordance with his or her mental strength and how the entire topic has been understood. This is continued until one has reached a point of necessary agreement. These audible debates and discussions are more beneficial than doing so quietly because that which is said out loud at the time of debate helps the mind. Additionally, many things will be apparent to a person speaking audibly that will not be apparent when done inaudibly. This is because of the comfortability that one's mind finds when studying quietly.

This is supported by something that has been narrated to me, and that is al-Sayyid al-Shareef, may Allah preserve his secret, traveled once to Egypt to study *mentar* under Shaykh Mubarak Shah. When he visited the gathering of knowledge, he asked Shaykh Mubarak Shah to give him an individual lesson so that he could learn Imam Razi's *Sharh al-Shamsiyya*. Initially, Shaykh Mubarak Shah did not accept his request and he put al-Sayyid al-Shareef with the other students. It was the habit of Shaykh Mubarak Shah that at nighttime, he would make his rounds walking by the rooms of his students to see their level of devotion and effort. He would also provide help to some of them if he noticed they needed it. When he reached the room of al-Sayyid al-Shareef, he heard within, the sounds of a debate, one asking and one answering, but the voice was the same. He looked into the room and saw al-Sayyid al-Shareef debating himself. He was acting as if he was debating Shaykh Mubarak Shah, by asking questions sometimes and answering them, and sometimes by giving answers on behalf of his teacher, or sometimes asking questions as if they were posed by someone else in order to protect the proper manners one should have with their teacher. When morning time had come and al-Sayyid al-Shareef went to class, Shaykh Mubarak showed him great honor and placed him in the front of all of the other students. He would also give much attention to the questions that al-Sayyid al-Shareef asked or presented to him. It is mentioned that the *Hashiya al-Sughra Laho* is actually written by him. It is said al-Sayyid al-Shareef wrote the text while he was studying under Shaykh Mubarak Shah.

It is necessary for the student to take a lesson from this story that whoever has the ability and aptitude for the like of this, that student should travel from one continent to the next, seeking out teachers and scholars and not become impressed with himself or herself and their own ability. One should never desist from seeking more knowledge through taking it from the mouths of perfected teachers. A true student's fear of his or her own inabilities and inefficiencies should force them to increase their knowledge, not only by studying the works of scholars, but also going directly to them and seeking the benefit that is gained by sitting with perfected scholars, meeting them, and keeping their company. That benefit is one which can never be obtained by mere study, even if it is an in-depth, comprehensive study done by a smart and hardworking student. Thus, it is necessary for every student seeking perfection to be aware of his or her own neglect and inability. In regard to others, the student should have high opinions, both of those preceding the student, and those that live in the same time, seeing in them perfection and superiority, never looking down upon anyone because of their speech or apparent understanding. We will speak on this in detail in the final advice and final chapter, God willing.

If one claims that the person who has gained the faculty of retention does not need to study the text and the words in order to gain more understanding, but rather that it should be sufficient to remember or recollect that meaning which has been firmly established and which he or she has retained, I would reply that, although the person who has gained the faculty of retention does not need to study the words to recall the field they have mastered, he or she does so to make it easier because human beings, so long as they stay in a state of growth and acquiring perfection, find it difficult to grasp meanings alone. Rather, they grasp meanings through the use of words or that which is similar to language in the ability to indicate meanings, like pictures for example. The human being thereafter digresses into the meanings of particulars by the means of contemplating and thinking about the meanings of generalities. If the human being needs words or something similar for grasping meanings for the first time, similarly he or she will need words or the like for grasping meanings the second time. The second conceptualization of meanings is called *tathakkar*, or retention because both of these have the exact same meaning. They mean that the human being can conceive or conceptualize that which is firmly understood by him or her for the second time and can separate it exclusively from all of the other meanings and ideas that have also been firmly established in their mind. The person can recall them by means of their memory. However, this recollection is a recollection of that which indicates to the meaning, i.e., the words or the picture. This is done either by the primary method, which is written words, or it is done by using one's mind or imagination. The recollection of these words or pictures is thereafter used to provide the secondarily sought after meanings.

There are two methodologies for recalling those things which indicate meaning (words or pictures). The first is the use of sensory perception, specifically sight or sound. The other is to use one's imagination. However, the former is easier than the latter.

By imagination or conceptualization, we mean to review those same words or signs while they are in one's mind. This, of course, is a very general explanation of what it means to imagine or conceptualize. The detailed meaning of conceptualization is that one breaks down an idea into isolated forms which are then stored in one's mind. Thereafter, one chooses from those forms that coincide with what one is seeking and then takes all of those forms and reorganizes them in such a way that they create a grander or more comprehensive form. This reorganized form should be harmonious with that which one learned in the beginning. Then, one uses that single general form as a method to recall the original meaning.

Without a doubt, this method is difficult, as it takes more work than the first (sensory perception). The first method is free from any strain or exertion. Due to this ease, one becomes comfortable and enjoys going from the meanings that have been retained, and digressing to the things that necessitate it because of those meanings. It also becomes apparent from these details that studying and reading has great benefit, for both one who has already retained information and one who wishes to increase in knowledge. Next, we should generalize the perspective taken regarding the definition of study to include all the forms of indication, whether they are written or conceptual, or we need to use the word "written" to include that which is written on paper and that which is written on the mind. In either of the two situations, we see that *mutala'ah*, or study, is a necessary component for retaining information. And, Allah ﷻ is the facilitator of ease.

A Final Word

Regarding Matters Which Benefit and Facilitate In The Attainment of What Is Sought After, From The Perspective of Perfection and Completion

It is necessary for every student to protect themselves from common mistakes and its sources. There are many reasons for mistakes and errors, so many that it is not possible to enumerate them completely. However, the majority of them return to one thing: not being able to differentiate between two similar things. This may be in regards to words and terms, or in meanings and concepts. Scholars have enumerated other prevalent mistakes and divided them into two categories: (i) the external mistakes, which are not directly related to the actual speech or written words, and (ii) the internal mistakes, which are directly related to words or speech. They did not go into much detail regarding the external mistakes because of the lack of benefit in knowing these, and due to them not being established and formed into a precise discipline. They did, however, divide the internal mistakes into those dealing with terms and those dealing with meanings. The mistakes relating to terms were further divided into six categories, and the mistakes relating to meaning were divided into seven categories. Thus, the complete number of internal structural mistakes that can be made are thirteen.

Regarding errors in terms, there are some related to individual terms, such as the definition of the term being equivocal or unequivocal, or the literal and figurative usage of words. The form of the word can be a form of *ilaha* (weakness) or a coalescent form. For example, take the word *mukhtar* (chosen), where the active participle is the same as the passive participle. Likewise, with the word *mudd*, the passive verb is the same as the command form. Lastly, the incorrect inflection of a word, or misspellings, can lead to misunderstanding the text. Other errors are in relation to sentences or phrases, such as a poorly constructed sentence. For example, if one says, *"Everything that an intelligent person conceptualizes is as they have conceived it."* Here, we see that the pronoun has the capacity of returning to the active participle or the passive participle. Another cause of mistaken understanding may be perceiving a single term as a compound word or vice versa. As for errors in meaning, some are in relation to the meaning of the preposition, either in both the subject and the predicate or one of them. This would be done by including something in the subject or the predicate which is not part of it. All of these will be labeled an incorrect syllogism. For example, one may take something which is an accident, and replace it with the subject or the predicate. This is called, "the fallacy of misplaced accident."

The next category of errors relate to the meaning of prepositions, which consists of mistakes relating either to syllogism or not relating to syllogism. As for those that are not relating to syllogism, one type of error is placing many questions within one question. This is called a "pact question," or a "complex question." For example, the statement *"Zaid is the only writer,"* which one may think is a single preposition, is in reality two prepositions. One of them is to affirm the skill of writing for Zaid, and the second is to negate that skill to anyone besides him. The fallacies that relate to syllogism will either be in regards to the forms of the preposition, or the subject and predicate of the preposition. Another type of fallacy is known as "begging the question," and it is to assume, or take for granted, or take as accepted, that which you are setting out to prove, smuggling the conclusion back into the premise. This is also known as "sophistry."

The fallacy that relates to the form of the preposition occurs when one assumes the form to be valid, when it is in reality invalid, due to an absence of some of the conditions of preposition. This is called bad or incorrect composition. In relation to the correct conclusions of the preposition, fallacies that exist are when the conclusion itself is one of the parts of the preposition, subject, or predicate This is known as *musaadarah*. If the conclusion that is gained was not sought after, it is known as an irrelevant conclusion or *ignoratio elenchi*. It is a form of circular reasoning and also referred to as placing that which is not a cause as a cause. These are the well-known errors and mistakes in acquiring knowledge, so it is necessary that a student learn them so they can protect themselves.

It is also necessary to beware of those mistakes which afflict intelligent students. They normally fall into one of two problems or a combination of both of them. The first of which is reading a text too quickly, and the other is constantly digressing from one thing to the next. As far as the first is concerned, when one's mind becomes accustomed to excessively fast reading, it becomes incapable of organizing knowledge learned. The mind also becomes incapable of differentiating between various types of information. Thus, the information which one has learned is confused and unorganized, like the dreams of sleepers. When one seeks answers from such a person, they are incapable of giving an answer because all of the information has not been given a form or order. Thus, such a person is incapable of expressing and explaining the knowledge they have learned.

The second one is digressing from one thing to the next and is harmful because the one who does so becomes accustomed to a lack of attention. He or she will constantly go from one idea to the next when there is even the smallest amount of association between the two, not taking into regard the true benefit of the original topic. Due to this, one is distanced from what one originally sought to obtain slowly, stage by stage. Thereafter, one does not have the ability to go back to the original subject, and if one attempts to do so, they will not be able to identify the train of thought that led to the initial progression of ideas. Such a person becomes more and more misguided and confused. We find them continuously drifting from one state of confusion to the next, and if this person continues and persists in this state, then they will become of those who are considered the people of compounded ignorance. This group considers their knowledge an intricate and deep one. If anyone asks them for some conclusive outcome or for any information, they will say, *"The answer to this is very complex, and not everyone can understand it"*, or a similar statement.

As for the one who has been afflicted with this and is aware of its danger and wants to rid themselves of this problem, they must be constantly mindful of their hastiness in study and must demand from themselves a summary and outcome for every question or topic they have studied, regardless of how short or long it is. They should not proceed forward until they have solidified that summary in their mind completely, and have made that summary the base, that everything is built upon. Next, they should build upon that base, being mindful not to go far away from that foundation. Everything that he or she learns secondarily that is connected to the foundation, they will add to that base, and when they study it again, that foundation, along with the new information, should create a new form or picture other than the first one. Then, they will study the connection between the two forms that they have just conceptualized and should not go beyond the secondary information until they have firmly understood the link between it and the primary information. They should not digress before completing this part of their study by investigating other topics. Investigating other topics before firmly grasping the initial subject will make one incapable of solidifying and understanding the information comprehensively. This will spread the meaning out of what one has learned in a way that will take them out of order and organization.

It is necessary for the researcher or student to not be hasty in their study. They should not move forward from one topic to the next before firmly establishing the first, nor should they move from one chapter to the next, or from one science to the next, until they have gained mastery in the first one. The primary cause for students not reaching perfection is precipitance and not being patient. The second cause for them not reaching perfection in study is the desire to learn another type of knowledge, or a book, for which the person is not ready. The primary cause of this is one's desire to raise their status in the sight of people and to gain acceptance from them. However, it is not conceivable that gaining retention ability in those sciences which one has gained a readiness for will be a cause for deprivation of perfection and a waste of time. True perfection is sought out by one making the knowledge that they have strong and ready not by a mere topical study of books or just reading with teachers without having understood them deeply.

It is necessary not to become accustomed to a mere memorization of words and expressions without comprehending the meaning of them. This type of retention will cause ignorance or stupidity. Researchers have explained that any mental faculty that is used over-abundantly, to the neglect of other faculties, will be strengthened, while others will weaken and diminish. These neglected faculties will thereafter become dormant, and the effects shall be seen. The purpose of study can never be obtained except by thinking and strengthening this ability. When memorization is strengthened, the ability to think is weakened, except, of course, if one's intention is to memorize some terminologies in order to reflect and ponder their meanings without being preoccupied in looking at the words. One should also be careful not to be accustomed to a superficial, shallow reading, which does not allow deep thinking. This can lead one to become a shallow scholar, like the storytellers for example. It is for this reason that students were prevented from studying books of literature and looking in the books of stories. They were also prevented from presenting to themselves secondary issues aside from the primary issues and proofs, because busying oneself with these issues can cause great harm to the student. The result of this mistake in learning is that one becomes a superficial scholar who does not have the ability to think deeply. The second, is arrogance and pride due to the general public's desire and concern with this type of knowledge. In reality, this is more harmful than the first harm.

However, a topical reading that is followed by a deeper reading and careful inspection is one of the necessary etiquettes of studying. Going into detail and depth after a general introduction makes knowledge settle more firmly. One must not accustom their mind to ease and comfort. Rather, one must exercise their mind and keep it moving and active for the majority of the time by keeping it busy with intricate topics and resolving complex questions. This is necessary because the mind, when it becomes accustomed to idleness, will, in the beginning, be a thing of choice, but it will lead to a compelled, irresistible state of idleness, which is what causes stupidity and ignorance.

It is also necessary that a student is not hasty and always relying on commentaries, marginal notes, or other writings to explain things because he or she is incapable of understanding the topic being researched. Rather, the student should persistently study the written works until he or she has figured it out for themselves, or he or she has given up all hope. Thereafter, they should refer to the books of commentary and explanation to compare what was derived with the books of commentary and the marginal notes. One may also compare their understanding to that which their teacher has derived from the work, in order to find out that which they were completely incapable of figuring out on their own. However, before reaching that point, by which I mean the point when one is generally incapable or unable to resolve a question on their own and reaches for a commentary, there is great harm, i.e., the harm of giving up on thinking and getting the mind used to inactivity. It is also necessary that one give up reading and studying when they see signs of boredom due to any of the causes of boredom. This is because the mind makes many mistakes when it is bored.

One should also refrain or desist from studying when their mind is busy with thoughts and different ideas that cause a distraction. One should also refrain or desist from studying at the time of hunger or when one is completely satiated, as well as when one is thirsty or excessively tired. Each of these states will cloud the mind and dull its ability to think. For indeed, studying depends on focusing one's thoughts and mind, as this leads to excellent understanding. It is necessary to take into consideration these things and protect from that which goes against studying. It is for this reason that they say it is necessary that one choose a time for studying that will be the best time for focusing thoughts, having a clear mind, and strong thinking. For example, the last third of the night, which is the best time for the things mentioned above.

One must be aware of not boldly entering into a debate before having studied sufficiently, even if it is a topic, which is clear to the person. Indeed, debate and discussion before studying does not produce anything except for loss and regret. Rather, before debating, one should not be complacent with that which was solely understood from individual *mutala'ah* and their own opinion. One should present their understanding to others, either by studying or discussing it with those whom they trust from their friends or by going it over with their teacher. That which will become clear with group study is much more comprehensive than that which will become clear with individual study. Group study is an activity of multiple minds, while studying in solitude is an activity of one mind. The individual seldom reaches the benefit which is attained by an entire group.

It is also necessary that one hold a good opinion regarding their pious predecessors and their peers. One should not look down on anyone regarding their speech or understanding. One should instead hold a skeptical opinion of one's self. One must be very careful to not become deluded by their own understanding and mental acumen. This will lead to him or her refraining from seeking out knowledge and participating in gatherings of knowledge. He or she will thus rely solely on their own ability to study the topics in which they feel prepared, placing complete trust in their own memory. Beware of this, because forgetfulness is a necessary accident of human beings. Lastly, one must be completely and absolutely careful to not have bad manners in regards to one's pious predecessors because this is a major cause of one being deprived of reaching perfection. We ask Allah for noble enablement and for good manners with our pious predecessors and our peers at all times.

Conclusion

An Explanation for Group Study And Some of Its Conditions and Etiquettes

Know that group study, according to the terminology of researchers, is defined exactly in the same manner as debating. The only difference is that group study takes place between two or more parties whose positions are not established, whereas debating is between two defined groups. In debating, one party assumes the position of affirmation and the other party assumes the position of negation. Whereas, group study consists of each participant taking turns supporting both sides of the argument. Group study often occurs between peers who share similarities and are at a similar level of knowledge. Whereas debating takes place between peers, associates, and others.

There is a notion that the difference between group study and debate is that debate refers to meanings, while group study refers to words and terminologies. This is incorrect. Our discussion regarding these two concepts is only taking into consideration meanings not in terms and the meanings that are derived from terms. As for the definition of debate, it is to investigate deeply from two perspectives, the relationship of things to bring forth and agree upon the truth. This definition is based on a subtle point mentioned in the books of debate. However, the reality is that debate is an exchange of diverging views between two individuals or a group of people who have investigated deeply. It is, of course, necessary that we include "an exchange in diverging views" in the definition of both debate and group discussion. True group discussion is when each person from the group mentions what they have gained from one perspective, after having individually reviewed or studied using all of one's mental capacities so that the truth may become clear to them. The benefit of group discussion is great if all of its conditions are found and its etiquettes are observed. It is even said that group discussion for one hour is better than reading and studying for a day. In fact, it is better than many days because reading and studying happens with one mind and intellect, whereas group discussion happens with many minds. The benefit of a collective effort over a single person's effort is self-evident. The benefits of group discussion are many and clear, not in need of explanation. However, these benefits are based on the implementation of conditions and observation of certain etiquettes. If these conditions are not found and these etiquettes are lost, then giving up group study is better because it will only lead to argumentation and fighting, which causes the truth to be lost.

From the conditions of group study are that the entire group be on the same level as people of good understanding and clear minds, none wanting to surpass the other or seek leadership over the others. There must not be any fights or argumentation between them, nor any foolishness or light-hearted joking. However, there is no harm if there is someone amongst them who is slow in learning and does not understand things except after much repetition and explanation. The harm that comes with this person does not affect anyone else, unlike the examples mentioned previously. Their harm will affect the entire group, and it will stop the attainment of truth and halt the benefits of group study and discussion. From its conditions also are that the individuals in the group have an affinity for one another, a familiarity amongst themselves, and no hatred or animosity amongst themselves because love will bring clarity, which in turn brings forth an understanding of intent or meaning, just as hatred causes the opposite of that. Familiarity also necessitates a delight or openness, which causes quick and good understanding, just as unfamiliarity causes a close-mindedness, which causes a loss of clarity of understanding and slow understanding.

Another condition of group study is that each person from the group know the vernacular of the other and understand their habits of expression. Each person's intent must be clear between them from the beginning, preventing them from unwarranted objections of each other's method. It is absolutely necessary for every participant in every group study or debate who is wise to avoid taking the position of the claimant, forced to provide supportive evidence. The one who this position places all difficulty and hardship upon themselves. Ease and comfort can be found in the position of questioning and investigation. In fact, the one questioning is in the easiest position and safest from the embarrassment of being silenced. Whoever wants good and ease from embarrassment and regret should choose the position of questioning and not see themselves as the final authoritative word on anything, even if they are, in reality, the authority in an area due to their research. This is because human beings are never free from regret and mistake. It is necessary for this person to portray themselves as a transmitter from someone else. All the while being doubtful about what they are presenting to the group. If it is possible for one to hold oneself back from coming forth and opening the door to a discussion, and one can wait until another opens the door, then one may take the position of questioning and investigating the other person. But if one is forced to open the door themselves, one should do so by indicating the general, basic aspects of the topic without any explanation or details. Then they will say, *"What do the brothers say or think about this?"*, carefully using gentle words and articulations with humility. This will incite love and familiarity in the discussion, whatever the topic may be. Then, they will quiet themselves in order to push away from the position of the claimant. However, if someone goes further by asking questions or investigating, and they seek firmly from them an explanation, then it is necessary for them to answer and face the questions in a way that does not make any type of a claim or necessitate a proof.

One should state everything as a transmitter, who is doubtful about that information and is not firm. This way, questions cannot be directed at them, and they cannot be forced to give conclusive answers. It is necessary to understand that the benefit of having a partner who has a comprehensive understanding is not less than the benefit of a good teacher. This benefit is gained through group study with that person. We used to hear from our teacher, may Allah open and widen his grave, that the blessing of studying with a partner who is blessed or has been given noble enablement over studying individually, is like the benefit of *salah* in *jama'ah* over *salah* individually. There is no need for further explanation in this matter.

When a student finds a partner or partners who are gifted, it is necessary that the student be conscientious of this person's feelings, and treat them like a sibling, or even more carefully than one treats their family. The student should be just with them in their group study and discussions. This includes all their dealings in seclusion or the presence of the teacher, or in the gathering of the class and in the company of people. We have surely seen many students who act justly and appropriately in the time of group study, but are reckless in the gatherings of people, leaving all justice, going down a path of recklessness and harshness. Rather, they become unmannered with their teachers when they are in the gatherings which are accompanied by the laymen. For this reason, the earlier generations of scholars would order students to first cultivate a good internal composition and good manners so that their bad habits do not become a cause for them to be deprived of knowledge and reaching perfection.

* * *

We ask Allah for His enablement for us to observe the etiquettes for the paths of seeking knowledge so that we reach the preservation of these etiquettes to our purpose. We praise Him in the beginning and the end, openly and internally, and we send blessings and prayers on our Prophet Muhammad ﷺ, the leader of the first and the last, his family, and companions who fulfilled the etiquettes of his companionship openly and in secret.

Indeed, the pen has taken a break from blackening these pages on the third of Rabi al-Awwal of the year 1124 AH. The scribe (Abdul Bari the son of Shaykh Nasr, the son of Shaykh Abdul Bari, the son of al-Haj Muhammad, the son al-Haj Abd al-Jalil, the son of al-Haj Abd al-Salam al-Ashamiya whose lineage goes back to Hasan al-Ashmaawiya. He is buried in the west part of the village of Ashma, located in the protected providence of Manufiya), completed this work to benefit himself and anyone Allah wills after him, on Thursday, 14th of Dhu al-Hijjah 1169 years after the prophetic migration.

May the best of prayers and the purest greetings be upon him, and all praise is for Allah, the Lord of the universe. May Allah, the most High, benefit us from the blessings of the author. Ameen, oh Lord of the universe.

Arabic Text

فيض الحرم في آداب وشرائط المطالعة وما يتعلق بها

تأليف

العالم العلامة المحقق المدقق الفهامة
أحمد بن لطف الله الولوي نزيل مكة المشرفة

بسم الله الرحمن الرحيم

الحمد لله الذي جعل الإنسان مستعداً لمطالعة الكائنات مع ما فيها من النفوس الظاهرة، ولملاحظة المصنوعات وما فيها من الآيات الباهرة وشرفه بجوهر العقل ليستدل به من العرض المحسوس علي الجوهر المقفول، ويتوصل بإعداده من المعلوم الى المجهول، الصلاة والسلام على أكمل المطالعين وأفضل الملاحظين سيدنا محمد خاتم الأنبياء والمرسلين، وآلة وصحبه المتشرفين بمطالعة جماله، المتأدبين بآداب كماله دامت الصلاة عليه وعلى صحبه وآلة

أما بعد

فيقول العبد الواثق بفضل ربه القوي أحمد بن لطف الله المولوي، غفر الله له ولوالديه وأحسن اليهما واليه قد كان يختلج في صدري، ويتردد في خَلَدي ان العلماء السالفين بَرّد الله مضاجعهم مع كثرة شَغَفتِهم وسعةِ مَرْحَمتهم في حق الطالبين حيث لم يهملوا شيئاً مما تُسَهّل طرق التحصيل عليهم إلا بينوه بدقائقهم ولم يتركوا أمراً مما يعنيهم في الوصول الي الكمال إلا ذكَّروه بحقائقه حتى دوّنوا آدابَ المناظرة والمباحثة وجعلوها علماً برأسه.

وألفوا فيه كتباً كثيراً من المتون والشروح والحواشي فما منعهم من ذكر آداب المطالعة وتدوينها علمًا كآداب المناظرة مع كون الأُولي أَهَمّ من الثانية في حق الطالبين لأن المناظرة متوقفة على المطالعة اذ كل مناظرة لم يسبقها مطالعة لا تنتج سوى المجادلة والمخاصمة ولا تثمر غير الخجلة والندامة فان

قيل تركوها احالة على فهم الطالب واعتماداً على أخذه تلك الآداب أعني آداب المطالعة من صنيع السلف في آثارهم من الشروح والحواشي اذ المطالعة اما في المتن او في الشرح قلنا لو كان تركهم لما قيل لكانت آداب المناظرة بالترك أولى وأنسب من آداب المطالعة لأنها مع كونها احط رتبة في اللزوم من آداب المطالعة ، أظهر فيها وأسهل أخذا من صنيع الشرَّاح وأصحاب الحواشي علي ان كثرة الشفقة تنافي الاحالة وتأبي عن الحوالة والجواب الشافي أن الأمور كلها بيد الله تعالي وهي مرهونة بأوقاتها وبينما أنا في هذا التردد اذ صادفت ورقة قد جمع في مقدار صفحة منها احد من العلماء المتأخرين عدةَ كلمات متعلقة بآداب المطالعة وكان أكثرها مأخوذا من آداب المناظرة لكنه من قبيل ما لا يشفي العليل ولا يروي القليل فكتبت عليه شيئاً مما استفدته من آثار العلماء وأخذته من أفواه الفضلاء وخطر ببالي أن أجمع مختصراً يحتوي علي آداب المطالعة وشرائطها على وجهٍ يفيد الطالبين ترقياً في مطالعاتهم ويعطي المحصلين كمالا في ملاحظاتهم ثم منعني من هذه الخاطرة عدة أمور منها تشتيت البال لكثرة الاشتغال وانقلاب الأحوال ومنها ملاحظة قصور الهمم في الطالبين ومشاهدة ما هم عليه من قصر الطلب علي ما يرغب فيه عوام الناس من الخشويات والدندنيات ومنها ما هو أمنع الأمور المانعة اني لاحظت قلة بضاعتي وعدم استطاعتي فقلت لنفسي ايها العاجز المسكين أين أنت وأين رتبة التأليف والتصنيف سيما يكون التأليف فيه قريباً من الابتداع

والاختراع حيث ما سبقك أحد فيه بتأليف مفيد ولا بتصنيف متبع حتي تستعين به فيما صعب عليك وتستكشف عنه فيما خفي لديك ومضي عليَّ زمان وأنا في هذا التردد ، اقدم تارة وأحجم تارة أخرى حتي جمع الله شملي بأن شرفني بجوار بيته الحرام

وضم الي الداعية المذكورة طلب بعض الأذكياء الكرام فبركة الجوار وصدق الطلب ترجح الأقدام على الإحجام وشرعت في جمع المختصر المذكور مستعيناً بالله الملك العلام ورتبته على مقدمة وخمسة مقاصد وخاتمة وذيل، سائلا من الله حسن الختام وسميته فيض الحرم ليشعر بأن ظهوره ليس بالاستعداد بل بمجرد الفيضِ والانعامِ والمسئول من فضله العميم وكرمه العظيم أن يجعله خالصًا لرضائه الكريم وأن يجعله نفعاً للطالبين وذُخرا لنا في يوم الدين بحرمة سيد الأنبياء والمرسلين، صلوات الله عليه وعليهم أجمعين.

المقدمة

في أمور تعين معرفتها في معرفة المقصود: منها معرفة المطالعة لغة واصطلاحاً، اعْلَمْ أن المطالعة في اللغة بمعنى الاطلاع يقال طالعته طلاعاً ومطالعةً اي اطلعت عليه وأما في الاصطلاح اعني في عرف عامةِ العلماء علي ما يُفْهم من موارد استعمالهم إياها فبالإجمال ملاحظةُ المرسوم لتحصيل المفهوم، وبالتفصيل ملاحظةُ الألفاظ المرسومة المعلومةُ الوضع لمعانيها للتوصلِ بها الي ما قُصد بإيرادها من بيان حقيقة أو إثبات مطلبٍ علي وجه معتبر عند أصحاب التحقيق، فهو علم يُبحث فيه عن آداب المطالعة وشرائطِها وموضوعُه المطالعةُ الاصطلاحيةِ وغايتُه صَونُ الذهن عن الاقتصار علي الظواهر والحرمان من الحقائق والدقائقِ والفائدةُ منه هو ترقي الاستخراج بمراعاة تلك الآداب وأما الغرض من نفس المطالعة فمختصر في أربعةَ باعتبار مراتب المطالعين، لان المطالع أي الذي له حظ ونصيب من استخراج المعاني من العبارات بمجرد ملاحظته ونظره فيها لا يخلو إما أن يكون ممن له استعدادٌ قريبٌ بالنسبة الي المحل الذي يطالع فيه وليس له علم بالفعل فغرضه من المطالعة ان يُحصل ذلك العلم أي العلم بالفعل واما ان يكون له علم بالفعل، بالنسبة الي المحل المطالع فيه لكنه تقليدي ليس بمأخوذ من الدليل فغرضه من المطالعة ان يُحَقق ذلك العلم بأخذه من الدليل وإما ان يكون له علم تحقيقي بالنسبة اليه لكنه في مرتبة ملكة الاستحضار

فغرضه من المطالعة ان يوصله إلى تلك المرتبة بتكرار أخذه من المأخوذ وإما ان يكون له علم تحقيقي لكنه مما يقبل الزيادة والقوة فغرضه من المطالعة أن يزيد عليه فينميه أو يأخذه من مآخذ كثيرة فيقويه ، فعلى هذا يكون الأغراض من نفس المطالعة أربعة أقسام إما التحصيل أو التحقيق أو الاستحضار أو التنمية والتقوية ولكل نوع من هذه الأنواع الأربعة للمطالعة آداب خاصة به كما أن لمطلق المطالعة آداباً عامة تعم جميع الأنواع ولهذا جعلت مقاصد هذا المختصر مُبينةً في خمسة مقاصد، وأما نفع هذا الفن فيعم جميع من له حظ من المطالعة إلا أن نفعه للمتوسط من الطالبين.

فإن طالب الكمال العلمي على ثلاث مراتب مبتدئ ومنته ومتوسط لأن الطالب إما في أوائل الطلب ليس له نصيب من المطالعة واستخراج المعاني من العبارات بملاحظته بل همه ان يأخذ مطلوبه من أفواه الرجال فهو المبتدي وأما في آخر الطلب فقد حصلت له ملكة تامه عامة يستخرج بها المعاني من العبارات الواردة عليه بسهوله من غير تكلف رَوِية جديدة فهو المنتهي، وأما في أواسط الطلب قد حصلت له ملكة الاستخراج لكنها غير كاملة تريد تكميلها بالتتميم والتقميم فهو المتوسط.

اعلم أن الملكة مطلقاً عبارة عن كيفية راسخة في النفس يصدر بها عن النفس نوع من الآثار الاختيارية بسهولة من غير رَوِيَّة ويقال لها قبل الرسوخ حال وهي كثيرة لكن المطلوب الكمال العلمي ثلاث ملكات مرتبة في

الحصول أولاها ملكة الاستحصال وهي كيفية راسخة في النفس تستعد بها استعدادا قريباً لقبول ملكة الاستخراج ويصدر منها بها آثار ملائمة لمرتبة استعداد الاستخراج وتحصل هذه الملكة بأخذ أوائل العلوم ومباديها الاولية عن أفواه الرجال وغايتها حصول ملكة الاستخراج وهي أعم الملكات الثلاث وثانيها ملكة الاستخراج وهي ملكة بها تستخرج النفس المعاني من العبارات الثلاث الواردة عليها بسهولة من غير تجشم رَوِية وانما تحصل هذه الملكة بإتقان الاصول من العلوم الأولية وباستحضار المهمات منها وتكمن بأمرين أحدهما ان تكون النفس في لاستخراجها بها متمكنة مطمئنة غير مترددة ومضطربة فيه وفي مطابقته للواقع ، وثانيهما أن تكون هذه الحالة أي التمكن والاطمئنان للنفس عامة في جميع العلوم المتداولة أو في أكثرها ، وكمال هذه الملكة بهذين الأمرين أي بالتعميم والتقميم إنما يتحصّل ويتيسَّر بالمواظبة على المطالعة بمراعاة آدابها وشرائطها وتطبيق المستخرج بها على مستخرجات الكاملين إما بمشافهتهم إن وجدهم في عصره وبلده وان لم يجدهم في بلده يختار الرحلة اليهم على سنن السَّلف وإن لم يجدهم أصلا لا في بلده ولا في غيره كما في عصرنا هذا كذلك إن الله و إنا إليه راجعون فبمتابعة آثارهم وتتبع مؤلفاتهم حقَّ التتبع وبالتأملِ في صنيعهم وفي كيفيةِ استخراجهم المعاني من العبارات وبعضها من بعض وفي دخولهم في المباحث وخروجهم عنها وتصرفهم فيها بالرد والقبول وفي تشعيبهم الكلام تشعيباً

مضبوطاً بحيث لا يخرجون به عن المقصود المسوق له الكلام وغير ذلك من آدابهم في التخريج ، ويدرج بهذا الطريق من علم إلي آخر فوقه بعد أن كمل استخراجه في الاول بالتمكين والتوطين ولما رأي العلماء أنّ حصول هذه الملكة وكمالها يتفاوت في الأزمان بحسب تفاوت الأذهان حيث تحصل وتكمل للذكي في أقرب الأزمان وأقصرها وللبَلِيْد في أطولها وأبعدها اعتبروا زمان حصولِها وكمالها للمتوسطين بين الذكاء و الغباوة وقدَّرَه بزمان قراءة كتب من عدةِ علومٍ متداولة علي أُستاذٍ كامل أو أساتيذ ماهرين ، وقسموا تلك العلوم إلي مبادٍ و مَوَادٍ وسَمّوا المنهي بها "مكمل المواد" وهو الكامل الذي حصلت له ملكة الاستخراج من تلك العلوم تامة وعامة وكملت من الجهتين وهو لا يحتاج بعد ذلك الي الاستاذ بل يشتغل بتنمية علمه وتقويته بالمطالعة والتكرار والافادة ، وثالثة الملكات الثلاث المطلوبة ملكة الاستحضار وهي ملكة بها تستحضر النفس المعاني والعلوم الغائبة عنها متي شاءت بسهولة من غير تكلف روية جديدة وتجشم مراجعة الي محلها من الكتب والرجال وانما تحصل هذه الملكة بتكرار اخذ المعاني والعلوم مأخذها حتي تتمكن وتتقرر في الذهن تمكناً بالغا الي الغاية المطلوبة وتكمل هذه الملكة كمالاً حقيقياً بعمومها الي جميع العلوم المتداولة واضافياً بالنسبة الي بعضها وهذه الملكة هي أخص الملكات واعلاها رتبة واعزها وجودا واكثرها رغبة فيها ؛ فاذا اطلق الكامل صرف الي صاحب هذه الملكة في جميع العلوم وهو في يومنا

هذا اعز من الكبريت الاحمر وكذا الكامل بالنسبة الي بعض العلوم كلما ذكر يراد به المستحضر في ذلك العلم دون المستخرج والمتحصل وإطلاق الكامل علي المستخرج التام العام مجاز باعتباران.

الاستخراج التام يوجد غالبا مع الاستحضار في أكثر تلك العلوم أو مع الاستعداد التام له في جميعها فينبغي للطالب أن يصرف همته في تحصيل ملكة الاستحضار في علومه ولا يقنع علي حصول ملكة الاستخراج ولو كانت تامة عامة فان الكمال هو الاستحضار ليس غير حقيقة واطلاق الكمال علي غير مجاز باعتبار كونه بعد الاستحضار ، ولا شك ان هذه الملكات الثلاث قد تكون بالنسبة الي مسئلة واحدة مثلا يحصل للشخص بالنسبة الي مسئلة واحدة ملكة استحصال ثم ملكة استخراج ثم ملكة استحضار كما قالو بمثل ذلك في المراتب الاربع للعقل إنها قد تكون بالنسبة الي مطلق العقل وقد تكون بالنسبة الي بعض العلوم لكن المراد من الملكات ههنا هي التي بالنسبة الي العلوم المدونة المتداولة بين العلماء فظهر من هذا التفصيل ان معظم المنافع من هذا الفن اعني من آداب المطالعة انما هو للطالب المتدرج في مراتب الكمال باستزادته يوما فيوما شيئا فشيئا وهذا الذي يعرب عنه بالمتوسط بين المبتدي والمنتهي إذ المراد بالمنتهي هنا من تمكن واستقر في استخراجه فيكون متمكنا في آدابه التي اعتادها في مطالعته وملاحظته فيكون انتفاعه منها قليلا ، ومما يعين في المقصود أن يعرف أن العلوم متفاوتة

في مراتب اليقين والظن فيجب علي كل طالب ان يعرف مرتبة كل علم في اليقين والظن لئلا يطلب من أدلته ما ليس في وسعها أو يقنع بالظن في ما يجب فيه اليقين ، ففي أعلي مراتب اليقين علم الهندسة فإن المستفاد من براهينها يقينيات في مرتبة الاوليات والضروريات ثم العلوم التي يستدل فيها بأدلة مركبة من مقدمات هندسية مثل علم الحساب والمساحة والجبر والمقابلة والهيئة المسطحة المبرهنة والموسيقي المسمى بعلم التأليف وغيرها من فروع الهندسة والحساب ثم الحكمة الطبيعية ثم الإلهية ومن الإلهية علم الكلام ثم ما يتفرع علي الطبيعة مثل الطب وأحكام النجوم وغيرهما ثم يتفرع علي الإلهية وهي أعلي مراتب الظن، علم أصول الفقه وفروعه المدللة بالأصول ثم علم النحو ثم التصريف والاشتقاق ، وأما علم اللغة فقد اختلف فيه فقال بعضهم أن اللغة ليس بعلم لأنها عبارة عن التعريفات اللفظية وأجيب بأنها تتضمن دعاوي فباعتبارها (هِي) علم ورد بأن تلك الدعاوي قضايا شخصية والعلم عبارة عن القضايا الكلية فخطر ببالي جواب لَعلّه غير بعيد وهو أنها دعاوي كلية مستدل عليها بالتمثيل كما في أكثر العلوم العربية وذلك أن في كل مادة من المواد المذكورة في كتب اللغة دعوي كلية صورتها كل ما يتركب من هذه المادة المرتبة مثل ضرب زيد مثلا في أي صورة كان موضوع لمعني كذا مثل الايجاع والايلام ثم يستدل عليها بالأمثلة الجزئية الواردة علي صورة شتيّ مثل ضرب ويضرب ومضروب وغيرها فتكون دعوى كلية قد استدل

عليها بجزئياتها على طريق التمثيل وعلى هذا يكون علم اللغة ايضا من العلوم الظنية المدللة فيها بطريق التمثيل كالتصريف وغيره من العلوم العربية فيجب على المطالع أن يراعي مراتب العلوم ويميز ظنيها عن قطعيها حتى لا يشكل الأمر عليه إمَّا بطلب المحال او بالقناعة على الظن فيما يجب فيه اليقين ، ومن العلوم ايضا ما لا يطلب فيه الدليل اصلاً بل غاية ما يطلب فيه صحة النقل ويسلم على سبيل حسن الظن مثل علم التاريخ والمحاضرات وفيه يمكن التحقيق والتدقيق بجهة مخصومة به يستعلم بتتبع كتب الأدب وتكرار النظر في نظمهم ونثرهم ومما يعين في المقصود أن يعرف أن لكل مبحث مبدأ ووسطا ومقطعاً ولكل واحد منها حق لازم يجب تأديته ، أما المبدأ فهو الدعوى أو ما هو بمنزلتها وحقه اللازم أن يحرر ويهذب بتعيين المراد من كل لفظ و بتعيين المذهب الذي تبني عليه الدعوى ليلا يقع النزاع اللفظ. وأما الوسط فهو الدليل أو ما هو بمنزلته وهو محط رجال البحث والتفتيش وعليه يدور السؤال والجواب وحقه اللازم أن يتأمل في مقدماته حق التأمل وكذا في صورته وشروطه كما سيجيئ حذرا عن المغالطة.

وأما المقطع فالمقدمة التي ينتهي إليها الكلام ويظهر بها المراد من الإلزام والافحام وحقه اللازم أن تكون مقدمته ضرورية مثل لزوم اجتماع النقيضين أو ارتفاعهما معاً وسلب الشيء عن نفسه وتقدم الشيء على نفسه وخلاف المفروض وأعظمية الجزء على الكل والدور والتسلسل وغير ذلك من

الضروريات أو يكون بمنزلة الضروريات لكونها مسلمة عند الجمهور كلزوم ارتكاب المجاز بلا قرينة او علاقة معتبرة او الاضمار قبل الذكر لفظاً ورتبة وغيرها من المسلمات عند أهل العربية وإنما وجب أداء حقه المذكور من كون تلك المقدمة ضرورية أو بمنزلتها ليظهر الحق وينقطع الكلام ، انتهي هنا الكلام إلي هذ المقام فلنشرع في المقصد والمرام مستعيناً من الله الملك العلام.

المقصد الأول

في بيان الآداب العامة إلى جميع أنواع المطالعين ؛ يجب على كل مطالع إذا أراد الشروع في المطالعة أن يذكر الله تعالى ويحمده وأن يصلي على النبي صلى الله عليه وسلم وأن يقرأ سبحانك لا علم لنا إلا ما علمتنا الآية وأن يقرأ ما في حفظه من الأدعية المأثورة الواردة في طلب الفيض وإلهام الصواب وأن يتوجه بقلبه إلى جانب الفياض المطلق ويتفرع إليه سائلا منه إفاضة الحق وإلهام الصواب وإعانته على تسهيل المطلب وتيسيره ثم إن كان شارعا في كتاب من فن من أت يتصور ذلك الفن بتعريفه المأخوذ من إحدى جهتيه ليحصل له علم إجمالي بذلك الفن ، ويتصور موضوعه أيضاً ليتميز المقصود عن غيره تميزاً ما ويتصور غايته والغرض منه ليزداد شوقا إلى تحصيله وإن لم يكن مبتديا به بل مطالعا فيه في محل مّا من مباحث الكتاب، وجب عليه أن يتصور المبحث إجمالا في أي شيء هو من المبادي أو المقاصد وما المقصود من ذلك المبحث من مبديه إلى مقطعه لأن كل مبحث يطالع فيه من له نصيب من المطالعة ، يجب أن يكون مشعورا به عند المطالع ، وإن أدنى راتب المطالعين هو الذي يطالع المحل لتحصيل العلم بالفعل وله استعداد قريب بالنسبة إلى ذلك المحل لا محالة وذلك الاستعداد يقتضي الشعور به ضرورةً مثل من يريد المطالعة في مبحث اثبات الهيولى ليحصل العلم بحقيقتها وإنيَّتها وهو يعرف

لا محالة أن عند الحكماء شيئا يقال له الهيولي وأنهم يدعون جوهريتها وثبوتها في الخارج وتركب الجسم منها ومن جوهر اخر حال فيها يقال له الصورة الجسمية ، وبهذا العلم الاجمالي حصل له شوقا الي معرفة حقيقتها وثبوتها تحقيقا وتفصيلا فراجع الي المحل المتكفل بتعريفها وبيانها من كتب الحكمة فبذلك يقدر علي التصور الإجمالي بأن المطلوب من الحد معرفة حقيقة الهيولي وثبوتها تفصيلا وتحقيقا ثم يشرع في ملاحظة المبحث تفصيلا ويبتدئ بتصحيح العبارة وتهذيبها بملاحظة مفرداتها ومركباتها شيئا فشيئا ليحصل له بملاحظة المفردات من جهة موادها ومعانيها اللغوية ملكةً في علم اللغة ويأمن بها عن الغلط والخبط من جهة اللغة ويظهر له المناسبات ووجوه المناسبات بين المعاني اللغوية والاصطلاحية وعسي أن يتولد من معرفة تلك المناسبات فوائد غير مأمولة بمنزلة النعم الغير المترقبة بحسب مراتب قوة الذهن وصفائه واستعداد النفس في استخراج المطالب بعضها عن بعض ومحصل له بملاحظة المفردات من جهة صورها وصيغها علي مقتضي أصول التصريف ملكة في علم الصرف و يأمن عن الغلط من جهة الاشتباه والالتباس بين صور الكلمات فإنه كثير الوقوع ويميز الفروع عن الأصول والمعني بالقياس عن غيره وعن الباقي علي أصله فيتميز بذلك عنده الحروف الأصلية عن الزائدة فعسي أن يستخرج من الزائدة معان دقيقة مناسبة للمقام فينمو عليه أو يتقوى إن كان من المستعدين لذلك وإلا فملكة

التصريف فائدة عظيمة في حقه سيما مع الأمن عن الغلط ويحصل له بملاحظة المفردات من جهة وضعها لمعانيها تميز الكل عن الجز والعام عن الخاص والمفرد عن المشترك واللغة عن الاصطلاح والحقيقة عن المجاز وبذلك يحصل ملكة في علم الوضع الذي هو أساس العلوم المتعلقة بالعبارة والألفاظ وإن كان يصرف همته في تحقيق وضع الكلمات والألفاظ حتى يعرف الوضع النوعي بجميع أنواعه الثلاث والشخص كذلك ثم يتأمل تطبيق وضع كل كلمة على نوع من تلك الأنواع ويتصور الأحكام المختصة لذلك النوع من الوضع انفتح عليه أبواب الدقائق والحقائق ثم يتصور المركبات من حيث هي مركبات وأجزائها من حيث هي أجزا المركبات وما يترتب عليها من جهة الأحكام النحوية والأحوال الأعرابية المناسبة للمقام ليحصل له ملكة في علم النحو أيَّ ملكة وينحل له التعقيد الناشئ من سوء التأليف ويأمن الغلط من جهة التركيب وهو كثير الوقوع، ويقع فيه غالبا من ليس له ملكة في علم النحو أو يهمل مراعاة أصوله وينكشف له وجوه المزايا والنُكات من المعاني التركيبية الزائدة على معاني المفردات وبعد انكشاف تلك المعاني إن شاء يسلك من جهاتها إلى المباحث الدقيقة ويجول في مضمار التحقيق إن كان من رجاله وفرسانه وإن لم يكن منهم فأيُّ فائدة تطلب فوق فايدة حصول الملكة النحوية ثم يلاحظ العبارة من جهة الخصوصيات التي بها يطابق الكلام بمقتضى الحال ظاهرها وباطنها وهي الحالات التي تفتضيها طبائع المعاني من

حيث هي معانٍ من ترتيبها بالتقديم والتأخير وتوصيفها بالتعريف والتنكير فيجب أن تكون الألفاظ الدالة عليها أيضًا علي ذلك المنوال والترتيب حتي ينكشف وجوه المعاني ويؤخذ منها بسهولة ولذا اعتبرها البلغاء وجعلوها مدار البلاغة وبهذه الملاحظة تحصل ملكة علم المعاني وذائقة الفصاحة والبلاغة فيعم المدار والوسيلة الي معرفة دقائق التفسير وحقائق القرآن العظيم، وبهذه الملاحظة أيضًا يعرف طريق صيد المعاني الوحشية العرضية اللازمة من المعاني المأنوسة الوسطية ويقال لتلك المعاني في عرف أصحاب المعاني المعاني المتصيدة ومن لم يألف بذلك وأهمل جانبه لا يعرف مناسبة الكلام لا للحال والرجال ولا للمقام ولا للمرام فلا يقدر علي تخريج المعاني الدقيقة المرتبة علي هذه المناسبات ثم يلاحظ العبارة بأنها هل فيها شيء من لطائف علم البيان مما تفاوت به وجوه دلالات الكلام علي معانيها الإلزامية والتضامنية في مراتب الوضوح، أعني هل فيها شيء من التشبيهات والاستعارات والكنايات ومن ساير أقسام المجاز وبالمواظبة علي هذه الملاحظة تحصل ملكة علم البيان وهي أعظم الوسائل إلي معرفة إعجاز القران وبتلك الملاحظة يظفر برقائق عبارات الفصحاء والبلغاء وبدقائق معانيها اللزومية والضمنية وبعد تمام ملاحظة العبارة وما يستفاد منها من المعاني الإفرادية والتركيبية والأصلية والفرعية والمطابقة والتضمنية والإلزامية ينبغي له أن يلاحظ المحل بالمعقولات الثانية أيضا أي الحالات التي تتعقل في المرتبة الثانية وهي التي

يبحث عنها في علم المنطق وهي تعرض المعقولات الاولي من حيث أنها موصلة إلي المجهولات فتلاحظ التعريفات أولا بأنها من أي قسم من أقسام القول الشارح هل هو لفظي أو إسمي أو حقيقي وهل هو حد تام أو ناقص أو رسم تام أو ناقص ثم يلاحظ أجزا كل تعريف فيميز الجنس عن الفصل والعرض العام عن الخاص والمفارق اللازم ، وأما التقسيمات فهي راجعة في الحقيقة إلي التعريفات فيلاحظ فيها هل هي من قبيل تقسيم الكل إلا الأجزاء وهو نادر في العلوم أو من قبيل تقسيم الكل ألي الجزئيات ويميز بينها بصحة حمل المقسم علي كل واحد من الأقسام في الثاني دون الأول ثم يلاحظها أنها حاصرة أو غير حاصرة وحصرها عقلي أو استقرائي ويتأمل في وجه الحصر ثم يلاحظ كل مركب من المركبات الكلامية الإخبارية بأنه من أي قسم من أقسام القضايا هل هي بسيطة أو مركبة وهل هي حقيقة أو ذهنية أو خارجية وهل هي حملية أو شرطية وهل الشرطية متصلة أو منفصلة وهل المتصلة لزومية أو اتفاقية وهل المنفصلة حقيقية أو مانعة الجمع فقط أو مانعة الخلوّ فقط ، وهل هي شخصية او محصورة وهل المحصورة مسورة أو مهملة وهل المسورة كلية أو جزئية وهل هي موجهة أو مطلقة وإن كل واحد من هذه الأقسام هل هي موجبة أو سالبة ثم يلاحظ نقيضها وعكسها المستوي والنقيض ثم يميز الدعوي عن الدليل فيشرع يلاحظ الدليل هل هو من باب القياس البرهاني والخطابي أو الجدلي لأن ماعدا هذه الثلاثة من الصناعات

الخمس لا يذكر في العلوم المعتبرة إلا نادرا وهو من قبيل الاستقراء، أو التمثيل أو الاستحسان أو استصحاب الحال أو غيرها مما يفيد الظن على ما يتحمله الفن وإذا تعين كونه قياساً يلاحظ أولا أنه مستقيم أو خلف اقتراني أو استثنائي مفرد أو مركب موصول النتائج أو مفصولها ثم يلاحظ بأنه من أي شكل هو من الأشكال الأربعة ومن أي ضرب من ضروب ذلك الشكل ويلاحظ شروط الشكل والضرب بأنها موجودة أو مفقودة ثم يلاحظ بأنه تام قد ذكر جميع مقدماته مرتبة أو غير مرتبة أو ناقص قد اقتصر إما على ذكر الكبرى لكون الصغرى سهلة الحصول أو على الصغرى يكون الكبرى ظاهرة ومشهورة أو على الحد الأوسط فقط لكون الدليل بمنزلة التنبيه ثم يلاحظ مقطع البحث بأنه على حقه اللازم من الضرورة أو التسليم أو ليس كذلك وبالمداومة على هذه الملاحظة يحصل له فايدة أيَّ فايدة ، أعني ملكة علم المنطق وهي ملكة بها يميز صحيح الفكر عن فاسده ورايجه عن كاسده. وكيف لا وعلم المنطق ميزان العقول والعلوم ومن لم يزن نظره وفكره بهذا الميزان لم ينتج قياسه سوي الخسران ومن لم يروض ذهنه ولم يهذب عقله به لا يخلو في أفكاره وأنظاره عن الخذلان وهو مقوم الأذهان كما أن النحو مقوم اللسان والحق أن هذين العلمين الشريفين بمنزلة الابوين المطالب في رتبته وإيصاله إلى الكمال فيجب على كل طالب أن يسعي ويجد لتحصيل الملكة فيهما بمراعاتهما في جميع مطالعاته وملاحظاته ولا يصغي إلى قول من نسب

تعلم المنطق إلي الضلال ويحمل ذلك علي جهله به أو علي تعصبه البارد لأن الإمام الغزالي رضي الله تعالي عنه أثبت في بعض مؤلفاته وجوب تعلم المنطق علي كل عاقل وهذا هو الإنصاف وبعد إتمام هذه الملاحظات اللفظية والمعنوية الأولية والثانوية يأخذ خلاصة المبحث ومضمونه من مبدأه إلي مقطعه ويصوره في ذهنه ويمكنه فيه بأن يقول مثلا حاصل المبحث وخلاصة الكلام أنه قد عرف العالم والحدوث أولا ثم حكم علي العالم بالحدوث واستدل عليه بالتغيير ومُنع تارة ونوقض تارة وعورض تارة ثم أجيب عن المنع بإثبات المقدمة الممنوعة أو بإبطال السند المساوي وعن النقض بمنع جريان الدليل في مادة التخلف أو بمنع التخلف عن المعارضة إما بالمنع أو بالنقض أو بالمعارضة ثم رد الجواب بطريق كذا وكذا فإذا قرر الخلاصة في الذهن يتأمل فيه من كل جهة ويدير فكره فيه كرة بعد أخري للإتقان وتحصيل الفوائد اللازمة من تكرار النظر وإن صعب غليه أخذ الخلاصة من المبحث وتقريره في ذهنه فهذه الصعوبة لها أسباب كثيرة منها ما هو لفظي مثل القصور في تهذيب العبارة وتحرير الألفاظ بتعيين المعاني المرادة منها ومثل الخطأ في تأليفها والأساة في تركيبها وعدم أعطا حقها من جهة النحو ومن جهة اعتبار الخصوصيات المعتبرة في المركبات ومثل كون العبارة في أصلها معقدة بسبب سوء التأليف من المصنف أو سبب ضعف القرأين والعلاقات الارتباطية وغير ذلك مما يقضي عسر الفهم وضعف الدلالة فطريق التسهيل

وإزالة الصعوبة في هذا القسم أي فيما يكون سبب الصعوبة لفظيا أن يكرر النظر والتأمل في تهذيب الألفاظ من جهة ذواتها ومعانيها ومن جهة تركيبها وتأليفها حتى يجد فيه منشأ الصعوبة والإشكال ويزيله ومنها ما هو معنوي مثل أن يكون المعني الحاصل من مجموع البحث معني دقيقا أو غريبا إما في نفسه أو بالنسبة إلى المطالع إما دقته فظاهر وأما غرابته فبأن يكون ذكره قليلا في الكتب بحيث لم يقرع ألا أسماع الخواص من العلماء أو بأن يكون له هذه الغرابة بالنسبة إلى المطالع وإن كان في نفسه معروفا مأنوسا لكثير من العلماء بحيث لم يقرع سمعه بهذه الصورة والأسلوب أصلا فيزول بتكرار أخذه من العبارة وملاحظتها بمعاونتها ومثل أن يكون المبحث طويل الذيل كثير الشعب إما بسبب أن يلتزم المصنف إثبات كل مقدمة نظرية بدليل مستقل بمرتبة أو بمرتبتين أو بمراتب فعلي كل تقدير من المذكورين تتكثر الدعاوي والأدلة وتختلط الأصول بالفروع وتتداخل الدعاوي والأدلة بعضها في بعض فيتشوش الذهن ويضطرب النظر بسبب هذه الكثرة مع الاختلاط والتداخل لأن الذهن يبسط ينفر من الكثرة إذا خلي وطبعه سيما إن كانت الكثرة مشوشة غير مرتبة فإنه أي الذهن إنما يدرك الكثرة بعد أن ضبطها بجهة واحدة بعد إن يلبسها صورة وحدانية بترتيبها ترتيبا معتبرا عن الميزانين وجعلها في حكم الواحد البسيط بذلك الترتيب المعقول وطريق التسهيل في كل واحد من هذين القسمين أن يميز الأصل عن

الفرع ويميز كل دعوي مع دليلها عن دعوي أخري مع دليلها ويرتبها علي الترتيب الطبيعي ولا يلتفت إلي الفرع قبل إتقان الأصل مع دليله وتقريره في الذهن ثم ينتقل إلي ما يليه طبعا ولا يلتفت إلي الوضع والذكر إن كان مخالفاً للطبع فيأخذ خلاصته ويقرره في الذهن كما فعل في الأصل ثم إلي ما يليه طبعاً، ويفعل فيه ما فعل في الأول ثم وثم إلي أخر المبحث و أيضا لا ينتقل من مرتبة إلي أخري قبل تقرير ما في الأولي من الدعاوي والأدلة والمراد من المراتب أما في القسم الأول فالمرتبة الأولي هي التي تشمل علي الدعوي ودليلها والثانية ما تشتمل علي أدلة مقدمات الدليل الأول التي أوردت في إثباتها والثالثة ما تشتمل علي أدلة الأدلة الثانية وهلم جرا إلي أن ينتهي إلي الضروريات إو المسلمات عندنا لكل هذا علي تقدير عدم تسليم الخصم وأما عند تسليمه بأي وجه كان فينقطع في الأولي أو في الثانية وإن لم ينته إلي ما ذكر.

وأما القسم الثاني فالمرتبة الأولي هي التي تشتمل علي الإنظار الموردة علي دليل الأصل مع إخوتها والثانية هي التي تشتمل علي الإنظار الموردة علي الأخوية أو علي ما في منزلتها وقس الثانية والرابعة عليها ومن أسباب الصعوبة تصور استعداد المطالع في استخراج ذلك المبحث فيسهي في تكميل الاستعداد ومنها أيضا كدورة ذهنه إما بحسب المزاج أو بسبب خارجي مثل هجوم الخواطر والهواجس فيؤخر المطالعة إلي وقت اخر لأن صفوة الذهن وجمعية

الخاطر مدار العمل، وأيضاً لكل وقت فيض خاص لا يوجد في غيره ، وأما إمارة أخذ الخلاصة من البحث وفهم حامل الكلام فهي أن يقتدر علي التعبير عنه بأي عبارة شاء .

وأوجز العبارات وأخصَرها إذا طولب به و سُئل بأن يقال ما حاصل الكلام وفَذْلَكَةَ المبحث وخلاصة المرام مثل أن يكون المبحث إثبات أن لكل جسم طبيعي شكلا طبيعيا مع الدليل المورود عليه فتقول في بيان الحاصل أن الدعوي إثبات الشكل الطبيعي لكل جسم وخلاصة الدليل أن الحد الأوسط هو وجوب التناهي والثابت به أولا مطلق التشكل ثم به الشكل الطبيعي وحاصل البحث والسؤال منع الكبرى من دليل المرتبة الثانية وحاصل الجواب إثبات المقدمة الممنوعة كذا وكذا إلي مقطع المبحث ويجب عليه بعد أخذ الخلاصة وتقريرها في الذهن أن يتأمل فيه من جهة الوارد والصادر وأن ينزل المصنف منزلة المدعي المستدل ونفسه منزلة السائل إن لم يتأدب مع السلف ويقول هم رجال ونحن رجال، أو منزلة المستفسر بأن يحاكي وظائف السائل عن الغير ويقول إن منع مانع أو نقض ناقض أو عارض معارض بأن يقول كذا وكذا ما يقول في الجواب إن تأدب مع السلف كما هو اللائق بل الواجب أن الفضل للمتقدم وأن كل من يستفيد من مؤلفاتهم من العلماء فهو أستاذ لنا وحق الأستاذ علي المتعلم معلوم ، كما سيجيء التفصيل في المقصد الخامس إن شاء الله تعالي وهذا أي القابل في الحاصل من جهة الوارد والصادر إنما يجب علي

من كان غرضه من المطالعة إما تحصيل ملكة الاستحضار أو التنمية والتقوية ، وأما من كان غرضه تحصيل العلم بالفعل وتحقيق ذلك العلم بأخذه عن الدليل ،فليس بواجب بالنظر إلي مرتبته وغرضه من المطالعة ومن كان له صفاء ذهن وجودة فهم وقوة قريحة بحيث يعتمد علي ذهنه في اقتداره علي الجمع بين الإيقان والإيراد فلا بأس أن أوجب ذلك علي نفسه بعد أن يحصل مقصوده الأصلي من العلم بالفعل أو تحقيقه وبعد أن يصل المحصل إلي مرتبة الاستحضار بالتكرار وإما بدون الاعتماد علي ذهنه أو معه قبل ما ذكر فتكون إبحاثه من قبيل الاشتغال بما لا يعنيه ومن باب ظفره النظام موديا إلي فوت الغرض وضياع المرام بل الواجب عليه ؛ أن يسعي في التحصيل والإتقان ويؤخر البحث والأيراد إلي مطالعة اخري وينبغي لكل مطالع أن يقلد في مطالعه المتون من كل علم شارحاً يثق به ويعتمد عليه في التخريج والاستخراج ويتأمل في صنيعه وفي أنه كيف يصحح الألفاظ والعبارات أولا وكيف يأخذ المعاني منها ثانيا وكيف يفتح البحث والتفتيش من جهة اللفظ والمعني ثالثا ، وكذا يقلد في مطالعة الشروح من كل علم محشيا مسلما عنده ولا يلاحظ كيف يتكلم تارة للشرح وتارة للمتن وتارة علي كل منهما وتارة يحاكم بينهما وإن لم يقدر مطالع علي جميع هذه الملاحظات كلها في كل مطالعة يختار ما هو أنسب و أهم بالنظر إلي المقام و إلي العلم الذي يطالع فيه وبالنسبة إلي نفسه ورتبته ويسال الله التوفيق والإعانة علي الزيادة ويقول

دائما بقلب حاضر في سره و علنيته رب زدني علنا بالحق والصواب وهو الموفق المعين لا يخيب السائلين .

المقصد الثاني

في بيان الآداب المختصة بمن كان غرضه من المطالعة تحصيل العلم بالفعل يجب عليه بعد أن أتي بالآداب التي مضي ذكرها في المقصد الأول كلاً أو بعضاً أن يتذكر أولا ما هو المطلوب عنده من العلم المشعور به في الجملة ثم يلاحظ المحل المطالع فيه هل هو مفيد وافٍ بمقصوده أو لا ، وعلي تقدير كونه مفيدا هل يفيد العلم التقليدي المجرد عن الدليل أو يفيد التحقيق المستفاد منه فإن كان الفن من الفنون الالية التي ليست مقصودة بذاتها مثل الصرف والنحو والمعاني والبيان والمنطق والأدب فلا بأس في الاقتصار علي التقليد التسليمي في الأوائل لأن مسائل تلك الفنون بمنزلة المبادي التصديقية ،والأصول الموضوعة للعلوم التي هي مقصودة بذاتها ومن شأن المبادي أن تسلم علي سبيل حسن الظن أو الجدل ثم في المرتبة الثانية وثواني الحال عند الترقي يطلب تحقيقها بالدلائل المناسبة لفننا ، وأما إن كان الفن من العلوم المقصودة بذاتها كعلم الكلام وأقسام الحكمة فيجب عليه أن يطلب العلم التحقيقي المستنبط من الدليل ولا يقنع بمجرد الدعوي والتقليد لأن الاعتياد بالتقليد والتسليم في تلك المطالب يورث الحرمان عن الوصول إلي المارب وإن كان المحل الذي يطالع فيه مجردا عن الدليل يطلبه من محل أخر بعد إتقان أصل المطلب بالتكرار فيتأمل ومقدماته وفي إنتاجه وإفادته المطلوب

حق التأمل ويلاحظ الوارد والصادر وفي دفعه كما مر في المقصد الاول ويجب عليه أن يقتصر علي مطلب واحد في كل مطالعه ويكرر فيه الملاحظة وقتا بعد وقت وحالا بعد حال بعد أن يصور مضمون المبحث من مبديه إلي مقطعه في ذهنه ويكرر التأمل فيه بدون اشتغال الحواس بنقوش الألفاظ وباستماعها وإن كان له عجز عن ملاحظة المعاني الصرفة المجردة فيستعين بتخيل النقوش الدالة عليها وإن عجز عن ذلك أيضا لشدة الألف بالألفاظ فيجاهر نفسه بالألفاظ ولا يقتصر علي لغة بعينها ولا علي لفظ المصنف وعباراته بعينها بل يعبر عن المقصد بأي عبارة كانت من العبارات الدالة عليه بالوضع وينبغي أن يكون حر المعني عنده بمنزلة صديقٌ قديمُ الألفةِ بحيث يعرفه في أي لباس رآه ولا تكون معرفته للمعني المتن مقصورة علي لغة أو عبارة مخصومة أو ترتيب مخصوص حتي إذا عبر عن تلك الصورة كان كأنه ما عرفه قط أو عرفه في الجملة لأن من كان يعرف معلومة بصورة مخصومة ويقتصر معرفته علي أسلوب واحد يقال له تابع السواد وهذه من موجبات الغباوة والبلادة بل من إمارتها ولا يخلط مطلبا مع مطلب أخر في مطالعته قبل إتقان الأول وتقريره في ذهنه وأن كان بينهما تناسب وتلائم في الجملة فان ذلك يشوش الذهن ويوجب النقص ويمنع عن الكمال إن كان صاحب هذه المرتبة صاحب ذهن قوي وهمة عالية أمكن له بيان يتدرج من تحصيل العلم بالفعل إلي التحقيق ثم منه إلي الاستحضار بالتكرار ، فلا

يحتاج بعد ذلك إلي مطالعة للتتميم بل للتنمية والتقوية فإنه قد وصل من الرتبة الأولي إلي الرابعة بقوة الذهن وعلو الهمة ، وأما إن كان إن لا يعتمد علي ذهنه في ذلك أي في جميع التحصيل والتحقيق والاستحضار فيصرف همته وسعته بحسب قوته إن كانت تفي بجميع التحصيل والتحقيق فقط بدون الاستحضار فيسعي فيها ويؤخر الاستحضار إلي مطالعة اخري وإن لم تف بجميعها أيضا فيجد في التحصيل وتقرير المحصَّل وتمكينه في ذهنه حق التمكين ثم يحققه في مطالعته اخري ثم يستحضره في الثالثة مع إعطاء كل مرتبة حقها ويحترز عن التكلف وتكليف الذهن مالا يطيقه فإنه يورث الكلال والملال قبل البلوغ إلي إكمال ونسال الله التوفيق والإعانة في كل حال.

المقصد الثالث

في بيان الآداب المختصة بمن كان غرضه من المطالعة هو العلم التحقيقي المأخوذ من الدليل يجب عليه أولا أن يتأمل في معلوماته وعلومه التي يريد أن يوصلها إلي مرتبة التحقيق بأخذها من الأدلة هل هي من العلوم الآلية أو من العلوم المقصودة لذواتها وعلي تقدير كونها من الأولي هل هي مما يقام عليه الدليل مثل مسائل النحو وبعض مسائل التصريف والمنطق أم هي مما يضبط علي حالة تقليدا وتسليماً ولا يقام عليه الدليل مثل علم اللغة فإنه قد اختلف في كونه علما فضلا عن كونه مدللا ، هذا في ظاهر النظر و إلا ففي الحقيقة هو علم يستدل فيه بطريق التمثيل كما سبق في المقدمة فليتذكر فعلي مقتضي الظاهر المطالع فيه ضبطه وإتقانه بأخذه من الكتب الموثوق بها من المشايخ الموثوق بهم وأن لا يشتغل بطلب الدليل لا شاهد وما علي موجب التحقيق فهو في مرتبة علم الاشتقاق والتصريف في تحقيقه بالشواهد والنظائر وتوجيه بالوجوه المناسبة ويؤيد ذلك ما ذكره ابن جني في الخصائص ناقلا عن أستاذه أبي علي الفارسي من أن اللغة يجري فيها القياس كما يجري في الاشتقاق والصرف والنحو ومثل ذلك بأنا إذا احتجنا إلي كلمة رباعية من مادة ضرب يجوز لنا أن نأخذ منها ضريب بطريق تضعيف لامه علي القياس المشهور في الإلحاق وإن لم يسمع ذلك من العرب قطعاً حتي قال في ذلك

الكتاب معرفة مسئلة من مسائل هذه العلوم العربية بالقياس والتوجيه خير من حفظ كتاب بمجرد السماع والتقليد ، فإذا كانت مطالعته في كتب التصريف والاشتقاق وما يتفرع عليها فحقه أن يطلب الوجوه المناسبة من وجوه المناسبات من المفصلات المتكلفة بها فيحقق علمه بها علي حسب ما يتحمله الفن من غالب الظن وإن كانت في النحو فيجب عليه أن يطلب الدليل والتحقيق بأن يراجع الكتب التي تتكفل بذلك ويمعن النظر في الجليل مهما يسعه الفن فيلاحظ أولا أن الجليل من قبيل السماع أو الأجماع أو القياس أو الاستحسان أو استصحاب الحال وينظر في كل واحد منها علي ما يليق به من النظر علي ما ذكره ابن جني واستوفاه في الخصائص وعلي ما لخصه الشيخ جلال الدين السيوطي في الاقتراح ، وإن كانت المطالعة في ساير الفنون الألية التي يجب أن يقام علي مطالعها الأدلة يطلب في كل منها علي مطلوبه من الأدلة أقواها ويتأمل في مقدمات الدليل بحق التأمل علي ما سبقت الإشارة إليه في المقصد الأول ، وإن كانت مطالعته في علوم لا يطلب فيها دليل أصلا مثل علم التاريخ و أيام العرب وساير المحاضرات والأدبيات من النظم والنثر فتحقيق إمثال هذه العلوم ضبطها وحفظها علي ما سمع وتدقيقها هو استخراج المزايا والإبكار من النظم والنثر واستخراج المعاني المجازية والكتابية العرضية ومراعات الخصوصيات والاعتبارات المتداولة المعتبرة بين الفصحاء والبلغاء و غاية ما يحتاج إليه في إمثال هذه العلوم هو الشواهد

والنظائر ليعلم منها اعتبار تلك الخصوصية عندهم وإن كانت في أصول الفقه ففيها مجال البحث والنظر واسع علي طريقهم المبين في كتب الجدل وفي أواخر كتب الأصول فيجب أن يطلب دليلا في كل مسئلة من مسائلها ويمعن النظر في الدليل وأما علي تقدير كون علومه من العلوم المقصودة لذواتها في ثلاثة أقسام قسم منها يطلب فيه الجليل علي كل مطلب منه ظاهرا وحقيقة سواء كان الدليل من العقليات الصرفة أو من النقليات والسمعيات المحضة أو مخرجا منها مثل العلوم الحكمية وما يتفرع عليها ومثل علم العقائد عند المتقدمين ومثل علم الكلام عند المتاخرين ومثل فروع الفقه المدللة بالأصول فيجب عليه أن يطلب في كل واحد من هذه العلوم ما يقضيه من الأدلة وإن يتأمل في الدليل بحسب تحمله .

وقسم منها لا يطلب فيه الدليل ظاهرا ويطلب حقيقة مثل علم التفسير فإنه لا مساس للدليل فيه بحسب الظاهر إلا إن كان معني يخرجه المفسر من النظم الكريم يطلب عليه دليل سمعي إما من السنة والحديث وإما من أصول العربية حتي يقبل منه ذلك التخريج ويسلم تفسيره من أن يكون من قبل التفسير بالراي فيكون لما يطلب فيه الدليل حقيقة وكذا علم الحديث فإنه ليس بحسب الظاهر للدليل مدخل فيه لكن المحدث إذا نسب الحديث للنبي صلي الله عليه وسلم يطلب منه دليل علي ذلك الإسناد الصحيح متواترا كان أو حادا مشهورا كان أو غير مشهور أو غير ذلك من أقسام الإسناد فإن

أسندوا أصل المتن إلي قائله إسنادا مقبولا معتبرا عند أصحابه قبل منه وإلا رد عليه ولم يقبل منه فكان علم الحديث علما يطلب فيه الدليل ويتكلم في دليله بالرد والقبول والتعديل والتخريج حقيقة علي ما هو مشهور عند مشايخ الحديث وأما علم أصول الحديث فهو من العلوم الألية وكأنه ملحق بأصول الفقه وباب من أبوابه وقسم منها لا يطلب فيه الدليل لا ظاهر ولا حقيقة وهذا القسم يمكن اعتباره من العلوم الألية ومن العلوم المقصودة أيضا ونحن اعتبرناه من الأولي مثل التاريخ وساير علوم المحاضرات فإنها إنما يطالع فيها من هو من أصحاب الجد وهم الذين يطلبون كل ما يطلبون من العلوم لتكميل النفس لكونها نافعة في تكميل بعض العلوم النافعة مثل التفسير والحديث لا لكونها مما يتلذذ به أو لكونها مرغوبا فيها عند أهل الهوي من عوام الناس ؛ يكون من العلوم الألية الغير المقصودة بذواتها وقد مرت الإشارة إلي ما ينبغي للمطالع فيها وأما الفنون الجزئية التي يعد العلم بها من المعارف في عرف العلماء فكل واحد منها متفرع علي أصل من العلوم الكلية وراجع إليه في غالب إحكامه ليكون في الاحتياج إلي الدليل وعدم احتياجه إليه وفي أداب مطالعته تابعا لأصله ومن الله التوفيق في أصله وفروعه.

المقصد الرابع

في بيان الآداب المختصة بمن يكون غرضه من المطالعة تحصيل ملكة الاستحضار بالتكرار يجب عليه أولا إن يلاحظ المطابقة بين ما عنده وبين ما في المحل الذي يطالع فيه في الدعوي والدليل فإن وجد المطابقة فيها من جميع الوجوه فنعم المطلوب فان وجد المخالفة فهو أما في الدعوي أو في الدليل أو فيهما جميعا وأيضا إما من جهة اللفظ فقط، وإما من جهة المعني أو منهما جميعاً و أيضا كل واحد منهما، إما كلا أو بعضا هذه هي الاحتمالات العقلية إما احتمال المخالفة في الدعوي من جهة اللفظ والمعني كلا فساقط إلا عند الغلط وإما من جهة اللفظ فقط كلا أو بعضا فجائز، وإما من جهة المعني فقط فساقط أو بعضاً فجائز، وإما في الدليل من جهتيها جميعا كلا أو بعضاً فجائز إذ يجوز أن يثبت مطلب واحد بأدلة وكذا من جهة اللفظ فقط أو من جهة المعني فقط كلا أو بعضا جائز، وإما فيهما جميعا من جهة اللفظ فقط كلا او بعضا فجائز ومن جهة المعني فقط بعضاً أيضا جائز وكلا ساقط فإذا وجد المخالفة الجائزة في الجملة يتأمل في وجهها وجهتها حتي يظفر بهما ويختار الأوجه الأقوى منهما إن لم يرتفع الخلاف بالتوجيه وأيضا إن كان يقتدر علي استحضار الدليلين جميعا يسعي في استحضارهما وإلا فيختار الأقوى منهما فيستحضره وينبغي له أن يجد ويسعي لأن يجد في كل تكرار

للاستحضار فائدة جديدة من الفوائد الأطرافية اللازمة إما من جهة اللفظ أو من جهة المعنى أن يصيد في كل مرة من ملاحظاته معنى من المعاني الوحشية المتصيدية ليحصل له فائدتان فائدة الاستحضار وفائدة الاستزادة فيكون من المحققين المدققين إذ لا شك أنَّ المعاني لا تخلوا عن لوازم بعضها بيّن وبعضها غير بيّن بتفاوت الأذهان في الوصول إليها بسرعة أو بطئ أو بعدم الوصول لخفاء اللازم وضعف الذهن وبها يظهر الذكاء ومراتبه لا بمنطوق العبارة والمعاني المطابقية لأن كل من يعرف وضع الألفاظ لمعانيها يعرف المنطوق لا محالة على السواء فلا يظهر منه رتبة الذكاء وينبغي له أن يعرف أن إيصال المعلوم والعلوم إلي رتبة ملكة الاستحضار وإنما يحصل بالتكرار وهو يتحصل بطريقين احدهما طريق المطالعة مع الاستعمال والأخر هي المطالعة والملاحظة فقط لأن العلوم التي يريد استحضارها أما ألية غير مقصودة بذواتها فيكون استحضارها بتكرار المطالعة والملاحظة وبتكرار استعمالها في مواردها ومحالَّها مثلًا إذا أراد استحضار اللغة والاشتقاق والتصريف يطالع كتبها مرة بعد أخري ويكرر في كل عبارة ترد عليه بذكر موارد المفردات ووضعها لمعانيها ويذكر كيفية أخذ بعضها عن بعض وتذكر صورها الأصلية والفرعية والمعتبرة بالقياس وغيرها مما يتعلق بالتصريف وإذا أراد استحضار علم النحو يطالع في كتبه كرارا ويكرر تذكر أصولها ووجوهها المحتملة في طي عبارة واردة عليه ولا يهمل تذكر شيء مما يتعلق بالنحو من تلك العبارة

، وقس علي ذلك استحضار المعاني والبيان والمنطق كما أشرنا إلي ذلك في المقصد الأول ، و أما المقصودة بذاتها فيكون استحضارها بتكرار المطالعة والملاحظة فقط ولا مدخل فيها للاستعمال وتكراره فيجب عليه إذا كانت مطالعته في العلوم المقصودة بذواتها ويريد استحضارها أن لا ينتقل من مبحث إلي أخر حتي يستحضر الأولي استحضارا محكما وكذا من علم إلي أخر مالم يستحضر العلم الأول حق الاستحضار ويحصل له ملكة الاستحضار في ذلك الفن وقد اختلف في أن ملكة الفن هل هي مجموع ملكات مسائله أو ملكة أخري تحصل منها عند تمامها وذهب إلي كل واحد منهما جماعة والحق هو الثاني ويدل علي ذلك أن معرفة المحدود ليس عبارة عن مجموع معارف أجزا الحد بل هي معرفة مستقلة تحصل من مجموع تلك المعارف عند تمامها علي القول الأصح ومما يدل علي أصحية الثاني ويوضحها أن الكيفية المتوسطة الحاصلة من تفاعل كيفيات العناصر المجتمعة المتماسة المتصغرة الأجزاء وهي التي يقال لها المزاج ليست عبارة عن مجموع تلك الكيفيات المتفاعلة بالاتفاق بل كيفية مستقلة حاصلة من اجتماع تلك الكيفيات فمن سلم المغايرة هنا اضطر إلي تسليمها ثمة إن كان منصفا وتسليمها هنا ضروري فكذلك ثمة هذا و إن كان خارجا عن الصدد لكنه لما كان لمعرفته مدخل في توضيح المقصود ذكرناه إجمالا ، ولما ظهر أن ملكة الفن غير ملكات مسائله علي القول الأصح وجب علي طالب ملكة الاستحضار أن

يلاحظ نفسه بعد تحصيل ملكات مسائل فن هل حصل له ملكة الفن أيضا أو لم تحصل وإن كان قد حصلت له فنعم المطلوب و إلا فيتصور ما المانع من حصولها هل هو لقصور في ملكات المسائل أو هو سوء الترتيب بين المباحث فذا عرف المانع أزاله باي وجه وإما الفرق بين مجموع الملكات وبين ملكة المجموع ، أعني ملكات مسائل الفن وملكة الفن فهو أن صاحب الأولي بدون الثانية إذا سئل عن الفن لم يحصل له علم إجمالي بسيط شامل لجميع مسائل الفن وصاحبها مع الثانية أي صاحب ملكات المسائل مع ملكة الفن إذا سئل عنه حصل له علم إجمالي بسيط محيط بجميع مسائل الفن ويخرج إلي التفصيل حين شرع في الجواب شيئا فشيئا كان الفن عنده مسئلة كلية مشتملة علي عدة علوم وادراكات علي ما بين في كتب الحكمة واورد مثالا ونظير العلم الواجب بالجزييات فكان هذا العلم برزخ وواسطة بين العلم الكلي الإجمالي المحض وبين العلم الجزيء والتفصيلي البحت لا من هذا ولا من ذاك نعم إذا سئل الأول أي صاحب مجموع الملكات فقط عن كل مسيلة مسيلة من الفن يحصل فيه ذلك العلم بتلك المسئلة المسئول عنها ،وأما عند السؤال عن العلم فلا وليكن ذلك في ذكرك بل نصب عينك فإنه من المهمات التي بتفرع عليها فوايد كثيرة.

وقل رب زدني علما.

المقصد الخامس

في بيان الآداب المختصة بمن كان غرضه من المطالعة تنمية علمه بالزيادة عليه أو تقويته بتحصيله من طرق شتى وبأخذه من مآخذ عديدة أما الأول أي التنمية فهو متفق عليه بين العلماء، وأما الثاني أي التقوية ففي التصديق متفق عليه كالأول، وأما في التصور فقد اختلف فيه فذهب الأمام إلى أن التصور لا يقبل القوة والضعف وبنى على ذلك إشكالا بأنَّ المجهول مجهول دائما لا يقبل التعريف واستدل على مذهبه بإن الشيء إذا علم بوجه ما ثم علم بوجه آخر فيتعدد العلم ولا يتقوى إذ العلم بالوجه الأول هو العلم به والعلم بالوجه الثاني هو علم به هو غير الأول فتعدد العلم ولم يتقوّ وإذا كان الأمر كذلك لا يمكن أن يعرف شيء لأنه إذا عرف بوجه فالمعلوم ذلك الوجه لا الشيء المجهول إذا الارتباط بين الشيء المجهول وبين الوجه غير معلوم لأنه يتوقف على معلومية الشيء فيلزم الدور ورد عليه المحقق نصير الدين الطوسي في أوائل شرح الإشارات قال إنما غلط الفاضل الشارح من إنه لم يفرق بين المعلوم الملحوظ بالذات وبين المعلوم الملحوظ بالتبع فإذا تصورنا شيئا بوجه مّا فالمتصور بالقصد والذات هو الشيء لا الوجه، والوجه متصور ملحوظ بالتبع إنما يتصور الوجه ليكون مرة لتصور الشيء الملحوظ بالذات ثم تصورنا ذلك الشيء بوجهٍ أخر يتقوى تصور الشيء الملحوظ

بالذات بسبب تصوره وملاحظته في مرتين إحداهما بعد أخري وعلي هذا القياس يزداد قوة بزيادة مزايا الوجوه.

هذا خلاصة كلام المحقق وهو أدق و أحق بالقبول ،و أما زيادة التصديق قوة وكمالا فمتفق عليه إذ لا شك أن حكماء إذا ثبت بدليل ثم ثبت ذلك الحكم بعينه بدليل أخر زاده قوة وكمالا ثم وثم و إذا ثبت هذا فنقول يجب علي صاحب الملكة في فن أو في مسئلة بل علي صاحب العلم بالفعل مطلقا إذا طالع فيه أو فيها أن يجد ويسعي أولاً في تحصيل الزيادة بالانتقال الصحيح إلي اللوازم والأطراف والقوة والكمال بتحصيله من طرق عديدة و أخذه من مأخذ كثيرة ثم يتأمل في المبحث في تصوّراته وتصديقاته هل يرد علي شيء منها سؤال بوجه مّا أولا وعلي تقدير وروده هل يمكن دفعه أولا و إن لم يجد شيئًا واردًا أصلا فلا يخلوا إمّا أن يكون عدم الوجدان هذا القصور إما من القصور في ملاحظة أجزاء المبحث و إعطائها حقها في التحرير والتعبير في مفرداته ومركباته إما من جهة المعقولات الأولي أو من جهة المعقولات الثانية علي ما سبق في المقصد الأول و أما من القصور في استحضار المبحث بحذافيره و أطرافه وقيوده و شرائطه و أما من القصور في أخذ الخلاصة منه وتقديرها في الذهن وتمكينها فيه حق التغرس والتمكين فالتدارك في جميع ذلك هو تكرار ملاحظة المبحث إجمالا وتفصيلا لفظا ومعني وقتا بعد وقت وحالا بعد حال إلي ان يظهر المقصود بفيض الوقت أو الحال فإذا ظفر بوارد إما أوّلا

أو بعد تكرار الملاحظة ينزل المصنف منزله المستدل ونفسه منزلة المستفسر أو السائل كما مر في المقصد الأول ويجاهر نفسه بالكلام كأنه يستفسر عن الأستاذ مستدا وظائفا لسائل إلي الغير وحاليا عنه بأن يقول مثلا أن منع مانع بكذا إما تقول في الجواب أو كأنه يناظر خصما في مقابلته ثم يجيب من جانب المصنف بالاستعانة من بعض القرائن المقالية السابقة أو اللاحقة أو المقامية أو الحالية ويترقي في الحث والتفتيش والسؤال والجواب بحسب استعداده وقوة ذهنه و إحاطته بالإطراق حتي ينتهي إلي مقطع ضروري أو مسلم وهذه المجاهرة أنفع و أفيد من المناجاة لأن الذهن معتاد بالمجاهرة عند المناظرة فيظهر له بالمجاهرة مالا يظهر بالمناجاة بسبب الألف والاعتياد ويؤيد ذلك ما يحكي أن السيد الشريف قدس سره سافر إلا مصر ليقرأ علي مبارك شاه المنطق ولما حضر مجلسه طلب منه درسا مستقلا من شرح الشمسية للرازي أستاذ مبارك شاه فلم يجبه إلي مسئوله لاستحقاره في بادي النظر وجعله شريكا لبعض الطلبة ومعني علي ذلك أيام وكان دأب مبارك شاه أنه يدور في الليالي علي حجرات تلامذته متنكراً لينظر في جدهم وسعيهم ويمدهم ببعض حوائجهم ولما وصل إلي حجره السيد الشريف قدس الله سره سمع من داخل أثار المناظرة يسأل ويجيب والصوت واحد فنظر من بعض الفرج إلي داخل فراء السيد وقد جلس بالأدب يناظر الشيخ أعني مبارك شاه بطريق الاستفسار تارة يسأل محاكيا وتارة من جانبه يجيب محافظا للأدب في

السؤال والجواب ولما أصبح السيد وحضر المجلس أكرمه مبارك شاه غابة الإكرام وقدمه علي سائر الطلبة وكان يصغي إليه بعد ذلك في كل ما يلقي إليه ويعرض عليه ويحكي أن الحاشية الصغرى له قدس سره هي التي كتبها وقت القراءة علي الشيخ ، يجب علي الطالب العارف أن يتنبه من هذه الحكاية علي إن من له ملكة و اقتدار علي مثل هذا التأليف الجليل يرتحل من أقاليم إلي أخر لطلب الأستاذ والشيخ ولا تعجبه بنفسه بتلك الملكة الجليلة ولا يتقاعد بسببها عن طلب الزيادة والقوة بطريق الأخذ من أفواه الكاملين ولا يقتصر علي الزيادة والقوة الحاصلتين له بمطالعة أثارهم وملاحظة مؤلفاتهم ظنا في حق نفسه بالنقصان والقصور و اعتقادا بأن الفيض الخاص بمشافهة المشايخ الكاملين وبملازمة مجالس الأساتيذ الماهرين لا يحصل بمجرد المطالعة ولو كان المطالع مستحضرا فهما ذكيا و قادا انقادا فيجب علي طالب الكمال أن يسيَّ ظنه في حق نفسه بالنقصان والقصور ويحسن ظنه في حق غيره من السلف والخلف بالكمال والرجحان ولا يستحقر أحدا في قوله وفهمه كما سيجي في وصايا الخاتمة إن شاء الله الرحمن.

فإن قلت صاحب ملكة الاستحضار لا يحتاج إلى مطالعة الرسوم والنقوش لتحصيل المفهوم بل يكفيه تذكر المعني المضبوط عنده واستحضاره. قلت إن صاحب ملكة الاستحضار وإن لم يحتج إلى مطالعة النقوش في أصل الاستحضار لكنه يحتاج إليه في سهولته لأن النفس الناطقة ما دامت في هذه

النشأة لا تقدم على إدراك المعاني مجردة صرفه بل تدركها بواسطة الألفاظ وما هو بمنزلتهما في الدلالة عليها من الصور المحسوسة وتنتزع من المعاني الجزئية بواسطة المفكرة المعاني الكلية ولما احتاجت النفس في إدراكها المعاني أولا إلى ألفاظ أو ما هو بمنزلتها احتاجت إليها في إدراكها إياها.

ثانيا أيضا والإدراك الثاني هو التذكر والاستحضار لأنَّ كل واحد منهما عبارة عن إدراك النفس المعني المضبوط عندها ثانيا وعن تعيينها إياه من بين سائر المعاني المضبوطة عندها و استحضاره بواسطة الذكر والاستحضار، احتاجت إلى استحضار ما يدل عليه من الألفاظ أو الصور أولا إما بطريق الأساس و إما بطريق التخيل ثم يستحضر بمعاونتها المعني المطلوب ، استحضار تلك الدوال أي الألفاظ أو ما هو بمنزلتها من الصور منحصر في إثنين احدهما الإحساس والأخر التخيل لأن الإحساس أسهل من الثاني أي التخيل لأن الإحساس عبارة عن مطالعة النقوش المرتبة الدالة علي تلك الألفاظ والصور ومشاهدتها حال كونها منقوشة في القراطيس أو فيما يقوم مقامها ، والتخيل عبارة عن ملاحظة تلك النقوش حال كونها في الخيال هذا معني سطحي إجمالي للتخيل أما تفصيله فهو عبارة عن أن نراجع المفكرة إلي الصور الجزئية المخزونة في الخيال وتنتحب منها ما يناسب المعني المطلوب ثم ترتبها ترتيبا يحصل به مجموع تلك الصور المرتبة صورة وحدانية كانت هي عليها أو علي ما يماثلها ويقاربها عند أخذ المعاني منها أولا ثم يعرضها تلك الصورة

الوحدانية هي النفس الناطقة فبواسطتها تستحضر النفس المعني المطلوب ، أعني تنتقل منها إليه ولا شك أن هذا الطريق أعني طريق التخيل لا يخلوا عن كلفة تعمل واعتماد بخلاف الطريق الأول أي الإحساس فإنه خال من التكلف والتعسف فيكون أسهل وبسبب السهولة تتبسط النفس ويحسن تصرفها في المعاني المستحضرة وانتقالها منها إلي اللوازم والأطراف وظهر من هذا التفصيل أن المطالعة لها نفع عظيم في حق المستحضر المستفيد أيضا لسهولة الاستحضار بها على أن لنا إن نعمم الملاحظة المأخوذة في تعريف المطالعة ويجعلها بمعني ملاحظة الدوال مطلقا سواء كانت تلك الدوال الملحوظة مرسومة أو مخيلة أو تعمم الرسم إلي الرسم في القراطيس وإلي الرسم في الخيال وعلي كل واحد من التقديرين يثبت الاحتياج إلي المطالعة في أصل الاستحضار ومن الله التسهيل والتيسير.

الخاتمة

في أمور تنفع معرفتها في المقصود من جهة التكميل والتتميم ينبغي لكل مطالع أن يحترز عن مواقع الغلط وأسبابه ومنشائه وللفظ أسباب كثيرة تكاد أن لا تنضبط ومع كثرتها ترجع إلي معني واحد وهو عدم الفرق بين الشيء وشبيهه في اللفظ أو في المعني ثم إن المحققين حصروا والمشهور الكثير الوقوع منها في قسمين خارجي ليس في نفس الكلام وداخلي في نفس الكلام ولم يتعرضوا للخارجي لعدم النفع في معرفته ولعدم انضباطه بضابطه ثم تسموا الداخلي إلي لفظي ومعنوي ثم اللفظي إلي ستة أقسام والمعنوي إلي سبعة فصَارت الأسباب الداخلية للغلط بحسب الاستقراء ثلاثة عشر سببا ومن اللفظي ما يرجع إلي المفرد إما من جهة وضعه وذاته مثل الاشتراك والحقيقة والمجاز و أما من جهة صورته الإعلالية مثل مختار اسم فاعل ومفعول أو الإدغامية مد ماضياً مجهولا وامرا حاضرا و أما من جهة إعرابه مثل المرفوع بالمرفوع أو من جهة إعجامه مثل المصحفات ومنه ما يرجع إلي المركب إما من جهة التركيب نفسه كما إذا قلنا كل ما يتصوره العاقل فهو كما يتصوره فيحتمل ضمير هو أن يرجع إلي العاقل أو المعقول و أما من جهة أن يظن ما هو المفرد في الحقيقة مركبا أو بالعكس ومن المعنوي ما يرجع إلي معني القضية أما من جهة جزييها جميعا أي الموضوع والمجهول مما هو داخل فيه أو

يعتبر فيه ما ليس منه ويقال لكل واحد منهما سوء اعتبار الحمل ومثل أن يؤخذ بدل الموضوع أو المحمول ما هو من عوارضه أو من معروضاته ويقال لهذا أخذ ما بالعرض ومنه ما يرجع إلى معنى المركب من القضايا قياسا كان أو غير قياس أما الذي يرجع إلى المعنى المركب غير القياس فيقال له إدخال سائل في مسئلة مثل أن يقال زيد كاتب وحده ويظن أنه قضية واحدة مع أنه مشتمل على قضيتين أحدهما تثبت فيها الكتابة لزيد والأخرى تسلب فيها الكتابة عما عداه و أما الذي يرجع إلى معنى القياس إما من جهة مادته بأن يكون شبيهة باليقينيات وليس منها أو بالمسلمات وليست منها فيقال لهذا سفسطة ومشاغبة و أما من جهة صورته بأن ترى صحيحة وهي فاسدة حقيقية لفوات بعض شروطها ويقال له سوء التأليف والتبكيت أيضا إما من جهة نسبته إلى النتيجة مثل أن تكون النتيجة عين إحدى المقدمتين أو جزؤها ويقال له مصادرة ومثل أن تكون النتيجة المستفادة غير مطلوبة ويقال له وضع ما ليس بعلة علة هذه هي الأسباب المشهورة بالغلط فيجب أن يستحضرها الطالب للتوقي والاحتراز عنها وينبغي لكل طالب أن يحترز من الورطة التي يقع فيها غالبا الأذكياء وإنما يقع من يقع فيها بإحدى أمرين أو بهما جميعا أحدهما أن يعود فكرة بفرط السرعة والآخر أن يتبع كل سانح، أما الأول فلأن الفكرة إذا اعتادت بإفراط سرعة في حركتها عجز الذهن عن ترتيب المستحضرات وعن تميز بعضها عن بعض حق التمييز فتكون المعاني

المستحضرة أخلاطا غير مترتبة مثل أضغاث أحلام النائم فإذا طولب بالمال والمحصَّل عجز عن الجواب لأن تلك الكثرة لم تلبس لباسا وجدانيا ولم تفض عليها صورة الوحدة بسبب الترتيب حتي يعبر عنها ، وأما الثاني فلأنه إذا إعتاده بإتباع كل سانح لا يزال يسنح له من كل سانح سانح أخر بأدني ملابسة بينهما سواء كان له مساس بالمقام أو لا فيبعد بذلك عن المقصود بمراحل ولا يقدر علي الرجوع إليه و إن رجع لا يجد الطريق إليه فيزداد طلالاً و مازال ينتقل من ناقض إلي ناقض ومن ضلال إلي ضلال فإن استمروا صر علي ذلك، كان من المحررين الذين هم أصحاب الجهل المركب وهم يعدون ذلك تدقيقا وتعميقا فإذا طولبوا بالنتيجة يقولون هذا معني دقيق لا يفهمه كل واحد ومثل ذلك من الترا هات و أما من ابتلي به وتفطن لقبحه وطلب الخلاص منه فعليه المواظبة علي ترك العجلة في ملاحظتها و أن يطالب نفسه بالمال والمحصَّل في كل مسئلة ومبحث قصير كان أو طويلا ولا يتجاوز عنه ما لم يتمكن هو في ذهنه غاية التمكن ، ويجعل خلاصة كل مبحث أصلا و أساسا ثم يبني عليه ما يبني ولا يبعد عنه كل بعد وكل ما بني عليه شيء لاحظه ثانيا مع ما ضم إليه وثني عليه ثم وثم وفي كل ملاحظة مع ضميمته يحصل له صورة جديدة غير الأولي فيلاحظ الارتباط بين الصورتين ولا يتجاوز إلي فروع الفرع حتي يضبط فروع الأصل ولا يشعب الكلام شعبا يحجز به عن الضبط والإحاطة وينتشر به المعني ويخرجه عن حد النظام

والانتظام وينبغي للمطالع أن لا يتعجل في مطالعته ولا يتجاوز عن مسئلة إلى أخرى قبل إتقان الأولى ولا من باب إلى آخر ولا من علم إلى آخر حتى يحصّل الملكة في الأول والسبب غالبا لحرمان طالب الكمال عن الوصول إليه هو العجلة وترك الصبر والثاني والرغبة في مطالعة علم أو كتاب ليس له استعداد قريب بالنسبة إلى ذلك العلم والكتاب ، والباعث على ذلك غالبا طلب الرفع عند الناس وطلب إقبالهم عليه واستحضار العلوم التي له استعداد قريب بالنسبة إليها فلا يتصور أنَّ هذا الفعل منه يقتضي حرمانه عن الكمال ويوجب كون سعيه عبثاً وضلالا إذا الكمال المطلوب إنما يحصل بحصول العلوم الواقعية في النفس مضبوطة حاضرة عندها لا بإتمام الكتب بالمطالعة السطحية أو بمجرد قرائتها الحشوية على أستاذ بدون أن يفهم معانيها حق الفهم ويملكها ملكا صحيحاً، وينبغي له أن لا يعتاد بحفظ الألفاظ والعبارات بدون فهم معانيها لأن مثل هذا الحفظ يورث البلادة بنا على أن المحققين قد بينوا في محله ان أي قوة من القوى الدماغية استعمل كثيراً زايدا على استعمال ما عداها قويت تلك القوة وضعفت ما عداها وتقاعدت عن حركتها وإظهار ما في وسعها من الآثار ، ومقصود المطالع لا يتحصل إلا بأعمال المفكرة وقوتها فإذا قويت الحافظة ضعفت المفكرة إلا أن يكون مراده من حفظ بعض العبارات استدامة الملاحظة فيها والتأمل في معانيها بلا تشويش النظر في النقوش وينبغي له أن لا يعتاد

بالنظر الإجمالي السطحي الذي لا يقتضيه إمعان النظر وتدقيقه فإنه يوجب كونه حشويا ظاهريا مثل القصاصين ولذا يمنع الطالب قبل الرسوخ والكمال عن مطالعة الكتب الأدبية وعن النظر في كتب المحاضرات وعن الاشتغال بالفروع المجردة عن الأصول والدلائل لأن في الاشتغال بها ضررين عظيمين في حق الطالب أحدهما ما ذكرناه من كونه حشويا ظاهريا غير قادر علي التحقيق والأخر هو العجب بسبب رغبة العوام فيه وعتنا الجهلة به وهذا في الحقيقة أضرّ من الأول.

وأما النظر الجمالي الذي يعقبه تعميق النظر والإمعان فهو من جملة الآداب الواجبة المراعاة لأن التفصيل بعد الإجمال أوقع في النفوس وينبغي له أن لا يعود فكره بالدعة والراحة بل يروضه ويحركه في أغلب الاوقات بأن يستعمله في المباحث الدقيقة والمسائل العميقة لأن المفكرة إذا اعتادت بالسكون أدي هذا السكون الاختياري في أوله إلي الاضطراري في أخره وهو يوجب البلادة والغباوة لأن محل المفكرة علي ما بين في محله هو التجويف الأوسط من الدماغ فإذا سكنت وتقاعدت عن الحركة زمانا مديدا امتلأ ذلك المحل بالبخار الكدارة الغليظ بحيث تعجز المفكرة عن حركة عند إرادة الحركة إذا كثر ،وكثف ذلك البخار فتقاعدت المفكرة اضطرارا أمّا بالكلية أو عن الحركة المعتدلة النافعة في تحصيل المطلوب بها ، وينبغي له أن لا يتعجل إلي المراجعة إلي الشروح أو إلي الحواشي والتحريرات إذا عجز في الجملة عن استخراج

المحل بل يلاحظه وقتا بعد وقت حتى يظهر عليه أثار المقصود والعجز التام عن دركة ثم يراجع إلي ما يراجع إما لتطبيق مستخرجه علي ما في الشروح وما في الحواشي أو علي مستخرج أستاذه ، و أما للاستعلام عن ظهور العجز التام ، وأما قبل ذلك أعني عند العجز في الجملة ففي المراجعة ضرر مثل ضرر ترك الفكر علي حاله وتعويده بالسكون وينبغي له أن يترك المطالعة عند ظهور الكلال والملال بسبب من الأسباب لأن الذهن إذا كل وملّ أخطأ كثيرا ، و أن يتركها أيضا عند اشتغال البال ببعض الخواطر الضرورية أو ببعض الحسبات والوهميات وعند تفرقه وتشتته ببعض المذكورات وعند الشبع والجوع والعطش والسهر المفرط لأن كل واحد منها مشوش للذهن ومفرق للبال والمدار في المطالعة علي جمعية الخاطر وصفاء الذهن وجودة الفهم فيجب مراعاتها والاحتراز عما يضادها ولذلك قالوا ينبغي أن يختار للمطالعة وقتا يكون فيه جمعية الخاطر وصفا الذهن وقوة الفكر أزيد من سائر الأوقات مثل الثلث الأخير من الليل فإنه أجمع للأمور المذكورة من غيره ، وينبغي له أن لا يتجاسر علي المناظرة قبل المطالعة وإن كان المحل عنده أظهر ما يكون فإن المناظرة قبل المطالعة لا تثمر غالباً سوي الخجلة والندامة و أن لا يصر علي ما استقر عليه رأيه وتمكن فيه فكره عند المطالعة قبل عرضه أما بطريق المذاكرة علي من يثق بفهمه من أقرانه أو بطريق المدارسة علي أستاذه فإن الغالب أن يظهر بالمذاكرة ما لا يظهر بالمطالعة إذ المذاكرة بتعاون

العقول والمطالعة بعقل واحد والمنفرد لا يدرك فضيلة الجماعة، وينبغي له أن يحسن ظنه في حق السلف والخلف ولا يستحقر أحدا في قوله وفهمه ويسيء الظن في نفسه، ويجب عليه أن يحترز كل الاحتراز عن أن يفتر بفهمه وذكائه فيترك الطلب وملازمه مجالس الأساتيذ ويكرر المطالعة في مباحث له فيها استحضار اعتمادا علي ضبطه وحفظه إياها إذ النسيان من لوازم البشر ويحترز غاية الاحتراز عن إساءة الأدب في حق السلف فإنه موجب قوي للحرمان عن الكمال. نسأل الله التوفيق علي حسن الأدب مع سلف والخلف في كل حال.

الذيل في بيان المذاكرة وبعض شرائطها وأدابها

اعلم أن المذاكرة في اصطلاح المحصلين علي ما يفهم من موارد استعمالها هي المناظرة الاصطلاحية بعينها إلا أن المذاكرة تكون بين إثنين فما فوقها بخلاف المناظرة فإنها تجري بين الشخصين فقط كما هو ظاهر من تعريفها وأيضا انَّ المذاكرة لا يتعين فيها منصب الاستدلال ولا منصب السؤال لأحد الطرفين كما يتعين في المناظرة بل بتناوب الكل في كل واحد من المنصبين، وأيضا أن المذاكرة تكون بين الأقران والأمثال المتقاربين والمتساوين في المرتبة بخلاف المناظرة فإنها تعم الأقران والمتفاوتين، وأما الفرق بأن المناظرة أنما تكون في المعني والمذاكرة في الألفاظ فليس بشيء فإن كلامنا في

الاصطلاحي من كل منهما لا في اللغوي وفي الاصطلاح كل منهما يقع في المعني بواسطة الألفاظ ، وأما تعريف المناظرة بأنها هي النظر بالبصيرة من الطرفين في النسبة بين الشيئين إظهاراً للصواب فمبني علي نكتة كما بيّن في كتب المناظرة و إلا فحقيقتها هي المدافعة بالكلام من الشخصين الناظرين بالبصيرة أو من جماعة ناظرين كذلك إلي أخره فيجب أن يقدر المدافعة بالكلام في تعريف كل واحد من المناظرة والمذاكرة فحقيقة المذاكرة أن يذكر كل واحد من المناظرة والمذاكرة فحقيقة المذاكرة أن يذكر كل واحد من الشخصين أو الجماعة ما عنده مما يتعلق بنسبة واحدة بعد أن يلاحظها بقدر وسعه طلبا لظهور ما هو الحق والصواب ، ونفع المذاكرة عظيم إذا وجدت شرائطها و روعيت أدابها حق قيل مذاكرة ساعة خير من مطالعة يوم بل أيام لأن المطالعة بعقل واحد والمذاكرة بعقول وفضيلة الجماعة علي الفرد أظهر من أن تخفي ،ومنافع المذاكرة كثيرة بينة غنية عن البيان إلا أن هذه المنافع أنما تترتب عليها عند وجود الشرائط ومراعات الآداب و إذا لم توجد الشرائط والآداب فتركها أنفع لأنها ؛ تؤدي إلي المراء واللجاج الموجبين لخفا الحق والصواب ، ومن شرائطها أن تكون الجماعة منصفين ذوي الأفهام الجيدة والأذهان الصافية لا يريد أحد منهم التفوق علي ما عداه ولا يدعي الرياسة عليهم و أن لا يكون بينهم لجوج معاند ولا سفية محرز ولا خفيف هزال ولا بأس إن كان فيهم غبي لا يفهم الكلام إلا بالتكرار والتفصيل لأن

ضرره لا يتعدى إلي الغير بخلاف من شرطنا عدمه فإن ضرره يعمّ الكل ويمنع الوصول إلي الحق وعن ظهور ثمرة المذاكرة عليهم ، ومن شروطها كون الجماعة متحابين متوا نسين لا متباغضين متوحشين لأن المحبة توجب حسن الإصغاء وهو يستلزم فهم المراد كما أنَّ المتباغض يقتضي خلاف ذلك و إن التأنس والتألف يقتضي الانبساط وهو يوجب سرعة الفهم وجودته كما أن التوحش يوجب الانقباض الموجب لسوء الفهم وبطية ، ومن شروطها أن يكون كل واحد من الجماعة عارف بلهجه الأخر واقفا علي عادته في التعبير ليتضح مراد كل واحد منهم علي الأخر من أول الأمر فلا يؤدي إلي المناقشة في التعبير ، ومما ينبغي لكل مذاكر ومناظر عارف أن يحترز عن جلب منصب الدعوي والاستدلال إلي نفسه فإن جميع الشدائد والمشاق في ذلك المنصب كما أن السهولة والخفة كلها في منصوب السؤال ، والاستفسار بل الاستفسار هو أسهل الطرق و أسلمها عن خجلة الإلزام والإفحام فمن يريد اليسر والسلامة عن الخجلة والندامة يختار طريق الاستفسار ولا يري نفسه قاطعا في شيء أصلا و إن كان قاطعا متيقنا فيه بحسب مطالعته لأن البشر لا يخلو عن السهو والخطأ. فينبغي له أن يظهر نفسه كأنه ناقل عن الغير وهو شاك فيما يعرضه علي الجماعة وإن أمكن له أن يمنع نفسه عن المبادرة إلي فتح باب البحث ويتوقف حتي يفتحه الأخر من الجماعة ويتعين له منصب السؤال أو الاستفسار وأن اضطر إلي فتح باب الكلام يشرع فيه مشيرا إلي

البحث واصله مجملا فيه لا مفصلا ومصرَّحا به فيقول ما يقول الإخوان أو ما رأيكم أو ما يؤدي مؤدي ذلك بتعبير لطيف يشعر بالتواضع ويحرك عرق المودة والألفة في المبحث الفلاني ثم يسكت ليدفع عن نفسه منصب الدعوي فإذا فصله الأخر بأثر السؤال أو الاستفسار وإن طلبوا منه التقرير والتفصيل ألبته وجب عليه أن يقرره بوجه لا يلزم فيه شيئا من الدعوي والاستدلال بل يقرر كل ما يقرر كأنه ناقل عن الغير وهو شاك فيه غير قاطع بحيث يتوجه عليه شيء من السؤال فلا يحتاج إلي كلية الجواب.

ينبغي أن يعرف أن منفعة الشريك الفهيم المنصف الموافق ليس بأقلَّ وأدني من منفعة الأستاذ الكامل في حق الطالب وهذه المنفعة إنما تحصل بسبب المذاكرة معه، وقد سمعنا من أساتذتنا وسع الله مضاجعهم كرة بعد أخري أن فضيلة الدرس مع الشريك الموافق أو الشركاء الموافقين علي درس المنفرد كفضيلة صلاة الجماعة علي صلاة المنفرد ، وهذا ظاهر كل الظهور لاحتاج إلي البيان فإذا وجد طالب شريكا موافقا واحدا أو ما فوقه ينبغي إن يراعي خاطره ويعامله معاملة الأخ بل أشد منها وينصف معه في مذاكرته وسائل معاملته في الخلوة وفي حضور الأستاذ ومجلس الدرس وفي حضور الناس لأنا قد راينا كثيرا من الطلبة ينصفون عند المذاكرة في الخلوة ويتقشفون في مجالس الناس ويتركون الأنصاف ويذهبون طريق الاعتساف بل يسيون الأدب مع أستاذهم إذا كان في المجلس من يعتد به من العوام ، ولذا كان

الحكماء المتقدمون يأمرون الطالب أولا بتهذيب الأخلاق حتي لا يكون سوء الخلق سببا لإساءة الأدب التي هي سبب الحرمان عن البلوغ إلي الكمال. نسأل الله تعالي التوفيق لمراعات الأدب في طريق الطلب حتى نصل بحافظ الأدب إلى الأرب. ونحمده في الاول والاخر والظاهر والباطن ونصلي علي نبيه سيدنا محمد سيد الأول والأخر وأله وصحبه المتأدبين بأدابه في الباطن والظاهر. قال المصنف قد استراح القلم عن تسويد هذه الوريقات في ثالث الثالث من رابع الثالثة من ثانية الثاني انتهي تنجيره علي يد منجزه لنفسه ولمن شاء الله تعالي بعده عبده عبد الباري بن الشيخ نصر بن الشيخ عبد الباري ابن الحاج محمد بن الحاج عبد الجليل بن الحاج عبد السلام العشماوي المنتهي نسبه لسيدي حسن العشماوي المدفون بغربي عشمة قرية بالمنوفية من إعمال مصر المحروسة وذلك يوم الخميس رابع عشر ذي الحجة سنة 1199 من الهجرة النبوية علي صاحبها أفضل الصلاة واذكي التسليم والحمد لله رب العالمين.

نفعنا الله تعالي ببركة المؤلف امين يا رب العالمين. آمين.

Acknowledgements

Our beloved Prophet Muhammad ﷺ has conveyed to us a tradition that is based on thankfulness and appreciation. When questioned about his ﷺ reasons for standing in the middle of the night hour upon hour, the Prophet ﷺ replied:

"Shall I not be a grateful servant".

I would like to take this opportunity to express my extreme gratitude to all those who have contributed to the translation of this text, and helped facilitate what you hold before you. Firstly, I would like to thank my beloved friend, Rushain Abbasi, without whom I would have never stumbled upon the original manuscript.

Secondly, Dr. Edmund Tori, whose suggestions regarding productivity and efficiency made this work a reality during my many bouts with writer's block. I would also like to thank Dr. Tori's daughter, Aasiya Tori, who worked hour upon hour putting together the initial draft. This work would not be here today, were it not for my beloved brother and friend, Adil Sayyidi's (Justin Cole) careful review and assistance with the text. I would like to thank my beloved wife who is a constant inspiration for me. Lastly, I would like to thank Muhammad Sattaur and the Imam Ghazali Institute for their support and assistance in bringing this work to fruition. All success is from Allah alone.

About the Imam Ghazali Institute

Without a doubt, the Islamic tradition is a deep and vast ocean of jewels. As Muslims living in the West, we have found ourselves often playing an important role in recent times: to preserve and protect our inherited tradition, while firmly establishing it for generations to come. The uniqueness of the Islamic tradition is one where each successive generation of scholars have received their knowledge from a verifiable chain of transmission. This has allowed Muslims in every generation the ability to trace the source. The Imam Ghazali Institute has been conducting Islamic education intensives of varying lengths since 2007 with the goal of reviving love and attachment to the traditional sciences of sacred knowledge.

The IGI Enrichment series aims to introduce English-speaking students around the globe to topics of unique interest often neglected. It is our hope that a student will go beyond a simple read of the text and seek out a teacher with who they can study it with, inshaAllah.

For more information about the Imam Ghazali Institute, please visit www.imamghazali.org.

About the Translator

Mikaeel Ahmed Smith is a teacher, writer, and activist. At the age of 18, he embraced Islam. Within a year after his shahadah, he learned to read Arabic and memorized the Qur'an. In 2008, he traveled overseas to study Arabic in Damascus, Syria. Upon his return, he continued studying the Islamic sciences in Buffalo, New York. In 2012, he completed his studies of the Sihah Sitta and Qur'anic Tafseer, earning his degree in Islamic Studies.

Other publications of interest

www.imamghazali.org

On Celebrating the Birth of the Prophet ﷺ
BY SAYYID MUHAMMAD ALAWI AL-MALIKI
TRANSLATION & NOTES BY RASHAD JAMEER
FOREWORD BY SHAYKH UMAR KHATIB AL-HADRAMI

This work of the late Muhaddith of Makkah, Sayyid Shaykh Muhammad Alawi al-Maliki, may Allah have mercy upon him, seeks to present the case for celebrating the birth of the Best of Creations, Sayyidna Muhammad, may Allah bless him and grant him peace. Al-Sayyid Muhammad bin ʿAlawi bin Abbas al-Maliki al-Hasani was one of the foremost traditional Islamic scholars of contemporary times, and without doubt, the most highly respected and loved scholar of the holy city of Makkah and the entire Hijaz region (Western Arabia).

Forty Hadith on the Virtues of the Testament of Faith
BY IMAM YUSUF AL-NABAHANI
TRANSLATION & NOTES BY DERRICK AHMAD PEAT
FOREWORD BY SHAYKH IDRIS WATTS
BIOGRAPHY BY SHAYKH GIBRIL F. HADDAD

In the stark realities and instabilities – both spiritually and physically – that we find ourselves floundering in, Imam an-Nabahani's summary of the virtues of the statement, "There is no god but Allah," allows us to recalibrate, to see clearly and stand at attention. In his presentation of the prophetic narrations concerning the shahadah, he reinvigorates its importance in our hearts, and like this, he calls us to observe its splendidness and empower ourselves with its benefits. The Imam's compilation is then not only a call to faith, but also a call to action, a signal to revive the proper understanding of our religion.

Forty Hadith on The Virtues of the Companions
BY IMAM YUSUF AL-NABAHANI
TRANSLATION & NOTES BY DERRICK AHMAD PEAT

Among Imam al-Nabahani's groupings of forty narrations, we find a collection concerning the stature of the Prophet's companions (may Allah be pleased with them). And how could it not be the case that we find the Imam presenting these narrations, when those blessed companions are the same figures who answered the call of their Lord and supported the Prophet ﷺ. The Imam puts this compilation together to remind us that Allah knows better of all such affairs and that our responsibility is to be pleased with whom He Himself is pleased with and to turn away from that which the corruption of our hearts and our negative assumptions may tempt us to delve into without knowledge or understanding.

Refutación de Aquellos Que No Siguen las Cuatro Escuelas
BY IMAM IBN RAJAB AL-HANBALI
TRANSLATION BY DANTE MATTA

For the first time in Spanish, Ibn Rajab's essay "Refutation of Those Who Do Not Follow the Four Schools" presents the case for the necessity of following Islamic scholarship. The essay covers several topics which include the historical development of Islamic scholarship.

al-Mursid al-Muin (Murshid al-Muin)
BY IMAM ABDUL WAHID IBN ASHIR
TRANSLATION BY DANTE MATTA

Al-Murshid al-Muin – the Concise Guide to the Basics of the Deen – is a widely recognized primary text for learning Islam in North Africa. In it the author, Abd al-Wahid ibn 'Ashir, summarizes in verse the three sciences of Islam, Iman and Ihsan: Maliki fiqh, Ash'ari 'aqida and tasawwuf.

al-Shama'il al-Muhammadiyya
BY IMAM AL-TIRMIDHI
TRANSLATION & NOTES BY ABDUL AZIZ SURAQAH
COMMENTARY BY SHAYKH MOHAMMED ASLAM

The Shama'il al-Muhammadiyya presents us detailed descriptions of the moral, physical and spiritual qualities of the Prophet Muhammad ﷺ. The perfections that Allah bestowed upon the Prophet Muhammad ﷺ: his outward physical form, his senses, his internal form and his inner beauty. No one can rival or outstrip him in any laudable quality or trait. He knows Allah as He should be known. He fears Allah as He should be feared. He loves Allah as He should be loved. Understanding the Shama'il is absolutely critical to any proper understanding of Islam, for it details the qualities of the message-bearer, which fundamentally alters how we understand the message he brought.

www.ingramcontent.com/pod-product-compliance
Lightning Source LLC
Chambersburg PA
CBHW070620300426
44113CB00010B/1597